THE
SINGULAR PREFERENCE
Portraits & Essays

PETER QUENNELL

THE
SINGULAR
PREFERENCE

PORTRAITS & ESSAYS

On entering the drawing-room she found the whole party at loo, and was immediately invited to join them; but . . . she declined it, and . . . said she would amuse herself for the short time she could stay below with a book. Mr. Hurst looked at her with astonishment.

"Do you prefer reading to cards?" said he; "that is rather singular."

PRIDE AND PREJUDICE

COLLINS
ST JAMES'S PLACE, LONDON
1952

To
Margaret Farquhar

PRINTED IN GREAT BRITAIN
COLLINS CLEAR-TYPE PRESS: LONDON AND GLASGOW

Prefatory Note

The essays collected in this volume were written for monthly and weekly journals during a period of more than twenty years. One, at least, originally appeared in 1930: others were published in 1951. For leave to reprint them, I am indebted to the Editors of *Contact*, *The New Statesman and Nation*, *The Times Literary Supplement* and *Lilliput*. My thanks are also due to those who have allowed me to quote from copyright material: to Mrs. Bambridge, Messrs. Macmillan and the Macmillan Company of Canada for permission to print extracts from *Debits and Credits* and *From Sea to Sea* by Rudyard Kipling; to Messrs. Macmillan, for the use I have made of *The Greville Memoirs*, edited by Lytton Strachey and Roger Fulford; similarly to the Clarendon Press, for *From the Chinese* by R. C. Trevelyan; to Messrs. Longmans Green and the author, for *The Unselfish Egoist* by Joan Evans; to Messrs. John Murray and the author, for *My Friend H.* by Michael Joyce; to Messrs. Allen and Unwin and the translator, for *Chinese Poems* by Arthur Waley; and to Messrs. Hamish Hamilton and the author, for *Rudyard Kipling*, *A New Appreciation* by Hilton Brown. Illustrations I owe to the kind permission of the following: *John Cam Hobhouse*, the Trustees of the British Museum; *Mrs. Thrale*, Picture Post Library; *Swinburne*, the Masters and Fellows of Balliol College and Mr. John Bryson, their Librarian; *Brummell*, Sir Owen Morshead, K.C.V.O.; *Balzac*, Madame Nadar and Messrs. B. T. Batsford, publishers of *Victorian Panorama*: *Coventry Patmore* the Trustees of the National Portrait Gallery.

P. Q.

CONTENTS

Saints of Literature

Three Dramatists

The Augustan Age

Regency Portraits

Victorians

Contents

Novels and Novelists

The Twentieth Century

Tail-pieces

Illustrations

Joseph Joubert

WHEN BALZAC declared that in literature " the important point was not to avoid mistakes but to have a quality that sweeps everything in front of it," not only did he describe his own achievement, which depended on the possession of just that triumphant and overwhelming quality: he also defined the choice that lies, more or less obviously, before every modern writer. Is he to descend to the market-place and seize the chances that it offers him, write profusely and often badly, endeavouring to learn by painful experience, hoping against hope that his talent is sufficiently tough and resilient to withstand the stress and strain of hack work, in the belief that the dangers of seclusion are ultimately more serious than those of over-exercise? Or should he remove himself from the odious hurly-burly, cherish his literary gifts in silence and in solitude, resigned to publishing at infrequent intervals so long as he is sure that nothing he now publishes will afterwards seem unworthy of the exacting standard he has set himself? To become an artist of the second category—a category from which such ruthless and reckless professionals as Balzac, Dickens, Shakespeare are, of course, excluded—a writer must combine extreme natural fastidiousness with an obstinate strength of character given to few human beings. If possible, he must have a private income, and (should that supreme advantage have been denied him) either an unusual capacity for making other people do his odd jobs or the vein of inherited puritanism that we see exemplified in the very different yet complementary careers of T. S. Eliot and James Joyce. Among writers who belong to the second group, Joseph Joubert established a record that still remains unbroken. For Joubert, besides being the most self-critical of men, the most exquisitely self-selective of European aphorists, seldom finished what he had begun to write and published nothing in his lifetime. He might have echoed Villiers de l'Isle— Adam's famous, and perhaps slightly fatuous, *bon mot*: " As for living—our servants will always do that for us! " His business was not to live—though on two occasions he basked in the autumn sunshine of a mild platonic love affair and, from good nature and a sense of duty, twice took public office—but to feel and reflect and discuss and, now and then, in a brief yet studied note, to attempt to capture the essence of his discoveries, emotional and intellectual. In short, he was one of those writers who prefer the un-sullied margin of the page to the cataract of words that defaces and obscures it: " I love blank paper more than ever (he wrote), and I no longer wish to give myself the trouble of expressing carefully any thoughts but those worthy of being written upon silk or upon bronze . . ."

Born in 1754, Joseph Joubert died in 1824, having served, perfunctorily but satisfactorily, as a local magistrate during the Republic and an inspector of schools under Napoleon, but otherwise whiled away his existence in leisure and retirement. Although the tendencies he displayed were manifestly " Palinuroid," he had none of the romantic intransigence of Virgil's fated helmsman and, to counter-balance his disdain of life, had inherited many of the solider attributes of the French provincial *bourgeoisie*. Paris often attracted him, and some of his happiest and most exciting days were spent there; but he had been born and brought up at Montignac in the Périgord, and spent much of his later life near Sens, in the little town of Villeneuve. He was an excellent son, a good father, a faithful and indulgent husband. His neighbours loved and respected him; and his frequentations in the Parisian great world never bred in him a distaste for simple country pleasures, the warmth of his own fireside, the beauty of farms and gardens. His mood was pensive and generally melancholic; and his melancholy coloured the landscape of his mind as an autumnal haze softens the outlines of some richly cultivated hillside, in the austere yet fertile region that during his impressionable youth he had known and loved best.

Strange that a man who thought so little of publicity, and avoided it all his life, should have made a friend of Chateaubriand, an artist who " wiped his eyes with the public " and, whether he exulted or wept, usually did so in the amphitheatre! Yet to the end they were close companions; and, after Joubert's death, Chateaubriand, with his gift of the evocative phrase, examined his old friend's personal genius and summed him up concisely. Joubert (he remarked) had been " *un égoiste . . . qui ne s'occupait que des autres.*" It was Chateaubriand's task, moreover, to read through, and make selections from the vast accumulation of papers that Joubert left behind him. The editor was already old, and, in another memorable phrase, spoke of the saddening murmur of the memories they called up: " *J'écoute derrière moi les souvenirs, comme les bruissements de la vague sur une plage lointaine.*" But he persevered; and a small sheaf of the *Pensées* was eventually printed for private circulation. Their success was unexpected; and since that moment Joubert's still small voice has gradually increased in volume, till we have come to recognise him as an exceedingly individual, highly gifted spirit, whose utterance winds its way like a delicate flute solo through an age of violence and discord. Matthew Arnold introduced him to English readers; and in the last twenty-five years a French scholar, M. André Beaunier, has written his biography, edited his correspondence and resurrected a mass of important new material from the pages of his note-books.

His English biographer[1], who acknowledges her indebtedness to the work of M. Beaunier, is concerned less with Joubert's importance as a stylist and a critic, than with his original charm as a human being and with the oddity of the experiences in which his peculiar temperament involved him. What those experiences lacked in adventurous variety they made up in intensity. Joubert's marriage was unromantic—a reflection of everything about him that was solidest and staidest: Madame Joubert was a good cook, and, no doubt, a very good listener. But during middle age he fell victim to a grand romantic passion. Or perhaps it would be more accurate to say that he did not fall, so much as allow himself to subside quietly and gracefully, laying his heart at the idol's feet with an urbane and philosophic gesture. The idol was Pauline de Beaumont. Like Joubert, she was *une âme bien née*: unlike Joubert, she was an aristocrat by birth as well as temperament and, although she belonged to a section of the French ruling class that had helped to prepare the Revolution, she had lost her home and friends—her father had been killed in the September massacres: her mother and brother had been guillotined— and, when Joubert first encountered her, she was sitting, alone and disconsolate, on the threshold of a peasant's cottage. Joubert was at once captivated. He pitied her delicacy, responded to her sensibility and admired the keen critical intelligence by which her sensibility was accompanied. Soon he was writing her long and tender letters.

[1] *The Unselfish Egoist. A Study of Joseph Joubert.* By Joan Evans. Longmans.

Expressions of love were kept under control, or replaced by a tone of affectionate solicitude. He implored her to care for her health and urged that she should overcome a dark strain of constitutional melancholy. " One must learn to love life," he insisted. And elsewhere: " I am well content to tell you that I cannot admire you at leisure, and hold you in high esteem as I should wish, until I perceive in you the most beautiful of all forms of courage, the courage to be happy."

Pauline de Beaumont recovered her faith in life—recovered it, at least, to the extent of falling violently in love with Chateaubriand, or " The Cat " as his friends called him in the little *salon* that Pauline set up in the rue Neuve du Luxembourg after her return to Paris. Joubert was pained but understanding. He did nothing so vulgar as to strike back; and, when he and his wife received an invitation to join the lovers at their country house, he brought with him a copy of Kant, a philosopher he detested, which he used to fortify himself against jealousy as he strolled to and fro along the garden paths. Pauline's image slowly receded, though he never ceased to write to her: that of Louise de Vintmille, who was as robust and sanguine as Pauline had been fine-drawn, imperceptibly weakened without entirely obliterating it. Again Joubert's passion was largely imaginative. He could not forget the silken rustle that her dress had made one momentous July day when they walked together in the Tuileries, or the scent of the great bouquet of tuberoses he had bought her at a flower-stall. Such were the impressions, such the emotional experiences, that Joubert really valued. Firm in his conviction that the life of the spirit was the only real life, that it was more rewarding to love than to be loved, that the pursuit of self-respect and peace of mind—" *son repos et l'estime de soi-même* "—must be his only guiding principle,

15

he could afford to discount, if he did not affect to despise, the facile successes of a romantic adventurer like Chateaubriand. He continued to appreciate his friend, but saw plainly all around him. And, as soon as the *Génie du Christianisme* appeared in every bookshop, Joubert composed several critical pages, the more devastating in their analysis because the style in which they were written was so polite and measured.

He lacks (observed the candid friend) . . . a kind of sincerity which one only has, and only can have, when one lives much with oneself, when one consults oneself, listens to oneself, and when this intimate sense has become very lively by the practice it has been given and the use that has been made of it. He has, so to speak, all his faculties turned outwards. . . . He does not speak with himself, he hardly ever listens to himself, he never questions himself, unless it be to discover whether the external parts of his soul, I mean his taste and his imagination, are content, whether the thought is well rounded, the phrases fine-sounding. . . . He addresses himself to others; it is for them only, and not for himself, that he writes; it is similarly their approval, rather than his own, that he seeks. Thus it follows that his talent will never make him happy. . . . His life is another matter. He composes it, or rather he lets it arrange itself, in quite another fashion. He writes only for others, and lives only for himself. . . .

Thus, in a few neat sentences, the contrast between Joubert and Chateaubriand—and between the types of character and the types of literature that they epitomise—is coolly, clearly set forth. Chateaubriand certainly lived for himself, and seemed to write for others: Joubert was content to plan his life with a scrupulous—maybe an over-scrupulous—regard for the obligations that he thought he owed to others, but, as often as he wrote, listened only to the advice of his own interior promptings and was satisfied, if he was satisfied at all, by the approval or applause that he himself awarded. But then we reach an uncomfortable dilemma. Chateaubriand's work set the pulse of Europe fluttering—a whole generation responded to his influence; while Joubert sat at home in bed, wearing a warm night-cap, expecting to " breathe his last in the middle of a beautiful phrase "—some phrase that he might or might not, as the mood took him, decide to commit to paper—or, with umbrella and muffler, pottered around the streets of Paris, absorbed in a continuous reverie, admiring the striped tulips or browsing at the bookstalls. Which was the more important of the two, the more valuable, the more praiseworthy? " Take your choice, and be damned to you! " mutters the sombre and haggard goddess who presides, with a saturnine smile, over the literary destinies of young men.

Gérard de Nerval

VERY EARLY on the morning of January 26th, 1855, in the *Rue de la Vieille Lanterne*, an ancient, sinister and filthy street behind the Place du Châtelet, an inanimate figure was found hanging from a rusty iron window-bar. Since the inhabitants of that part of Paris were reluctant to meddle in any affair that concerned a dead or dying man, they did not cut down the suicide until a police-patrol arrived; and, although breathing when he was first discovered, he was beyond hope of resuscitation before the noose was finally loosened. Shabbily dressed, pockets stuffed with manuscripts, writing materials and miscellaneous rubbish, the pathetic corpse was at length identified. Friends claimed Gérard Labrunie, better known as Gérard de Nerval. They also recognised the cord with which he had contrived to hang himself—a strong piece of unbleached apron-string which, some days earlier, he had proudly shown to his old companions, Théophile Gautier and Maxime du Camp, observing that he had just been lucky enough to purchase the girdle that Madame de Maintenon had worn at St. Cyr for the performance of *Esther*. To other friends he had exhibited it as the garter of Marguerite de Valois or the Duchesse de Longueville. His intimates were well accustomed to Gérard's eccentricities. The gentlest and kindest of human beings, he had passed several periods of seclusion

18

in Dr. Blanche's madhouse, from which, however, he had always emerged, his literary faculties unimpaired. The season was bitterly cold, and Gérard had no overcoat. But, as usual, he refused to accept help, producing a Louis XVIII gold coin with the remark that he had his week's expenses, then went out across the frozen snow into the dark labyrinth of mid-nineteenth-century Paris—a metropolis that, at least in the obscure and dilapidated quarters which Gérard most frequented, still bore a considerable resemblance to the grim and tortuous city haunted by François Villon.

There he lost himself both physically and spiritually. To an acquaintance met near the Halles he complained that he was involved in a story in which he could not find his way—so darkly and insistently were the shadows crowding round—and that he spent hours of perplexity trying to regain his bearings. With him he carried the proofs of the curious book he called *Aurélia*, his last attempt to explain the origins of his private tragedy by retracing the fragile yet indissoluble thread that he had been following since the days of his youth. Earlier and later poets have had much the same experiences; but no other writer—not even William Blake who condensed his visions or hallucinations into a hard-and-fast mythological system—has lived so consistently beyond the Horn and Ivory Gates and has taken so little account of the distracting demands of " real life." For Gérard, as for Blake, the existence of the imagination was the only real one. Yet, like Blake, he had an extremely practical turn; and he is interesting, not as a moon-struck visionary who produced a few enigmatic and beautiful verses and came to a catastrophic end, but as a man of genius who brought light, albeit a glimmering light, into some of the duskier regions of the human heart and intellect, pursuing his quest up to the very limits, and then across the verge, of sanity. His great sonnets have the quality of incantations, and exert a spell that seems to grow stronger, though not less mysterious, the more often they are re-read. But his finest story is simplicity itself. *Sylvie*, composed in 1852, when the shadows were already gathering, is a brief idyllic episode, a glimpse of the enchanted past, viewed from a distance down the long perspectives of his strange and troubled adult career.

Proust declared that it was among his favourite books—a preference easy to understand, since *Sylvie: Souvenirs du Valois* shows its author embarked on an imaginative expedition *à la recherche du temps perdu*, revisiting the places he adored, invoking the phantoms of the men and women he had loved best, and finding in their renewed vitality a proof that imaginative Recollection was yet more powerful than the insidious attacks of Time. The past lives in us: we are ourselves the past: what we have deeply experienced and truly felt is as real and substantial as the chaotic impressions of the present hour. Everything changes and passes: the artist's business, with the help of Memory, is to distinguish the recurrence of certain dominant themes that run through the confused pattern of emotional experience. It is those themes we must treasure and cling to. Have I loved many women, Gérard inquired; or was it always the same woman under several different guises? The nun—the peasant girl—the actress—was not each of them an avatar of the same divinity? And, that divinity being changeable and multiform, could he expect to grasp and enjoy her in any single human shape? The deepest pleasures are subjective, the only true rewards imaginative. Now and then Gérard grew impatient at his imaginative servitude, and commented wryly on his invariable knack of seizing the shadow and letting slip the substance. But, when he reflected on the course of his emotional wanderings, he was ultimately convinced that no other course lay open to him: for him the shadow was real and enduring, the substance false and transitory.

This conviction was no mere literary whim. Gérard de Nerval never abandoned it; and it continued to dominate his existence from his boyhood till his last days. When he died, he was not yet fifty. Born in 1808, he was the son of Etienne Labrunie, a surgeon with Napoleon's armies, who had also served and had twice been wounded in the Revolutionary Wars. Etienne survived to tell the tale, a brave, conscientious, somewhat unsympathetic personage; but Gérard's mother met an untimely death. Following her husband through the campaigns in Eastern Europe, she succumbed at the age of twenty-five to fatigue and hardship, aggravated by a " fever she caught while crossing a bridge covered with corpses where her carriage was nearly overturned." It is not impossible that regret for a mother he had never known, and resentment at the emotional deprivation her early death had caused him, encouraged Gérard's life-long cult of an elusive mother-mistress, embodied in the series of women whom he idolised but either failed to win or deliberately refrained from capturing. Yet his youth was cheerful and carefree. Brought up by his maternal grand-uncle in the village of Mortefontaine near the pleasant town of Senlis, he was reared amid reminiscences of the eighteenth-century philosophers—whose works he supplemented by a study of the Cabalists and *Illuminati*—in a landscape that recalled Rousseau and *La Nouvelle Héloïse*. Here he acquired his deep devotion to the Valois, its legends and its folk-songs; and the theme of *Sylvie* is a Parisian's journey home to the cradle of his youthful loves — to Mortefontaine and Senlis and Loisy, to the country of forests and lakes and sandy heaths, where he had paid innocent court to the virginal lace-maker and, on the threshold of a small lonely ancient *château*, in a ring of listening white-garbed children, had glimpsed Adrienne for the first time.

Already he was the prey of a further obsession. Adrienne's identity is doubtful: Sylvie was probably recollected from a certain Reine-Sylvie Tremblay, who married a local shepherd and died, just before the composition of *Sylvie*, in the autumn of 1852; but there can be no doubt that the popular actress, described in the opening paragraphs of the tale, was a solid earthy personage—Jenny Colon, a star of comic opera, a fair-haired, blue-eyed enchantress, with a small, sweet voice, a smooth skin and exquisitely rounded and dimpled cheeks. Gérard's infatuation was pleasurable agony. Night after night, he tells us in *Sylvie*, he attended the theatre " *en grande tenue de soupirant* "; but, although when the curtain went down, and the divine apparition temporarily vanished, he was invaded by an intolerable sense of loss—" *l'amère tristesse que laisse un songe évanoui* "—he feared to trouble Jenny's image in " the magical looking-glass," and was only persuaded to meet her face to face, by the rigorous insistence of his less romantic friends. True, he had purchased a bed in which to receive her; but, having set it up in the middle of his room, he placed his own mattress on the floor beside it, as upon the steps of an altar. Asked who slept in the bed, under its Renaissance canopy, between its twisted columns, he replied simply: " My imagination."

As a poet and story-teller and founder of the Symbolist movement, Gérard de Nerval has long been acclaimed by French critics. Barrès envied him: Proust saluted him: more recently he has had the questionable honour of a Surrealist *accolade*. To the English public the story of his life and literary growth is relatively little known. Gérard, in fact, had two careers. Besides being a visionary poet and a master of imaginative prose, he was also an industrious translator (whose version of *Faust* Goethe himself applauded, announcing that, now that he could no longer read his play in German, he found that the French rendering restored its novelty and freshness), an author of entertaining travel-books and a diligent professional playwright. In the second aspect he is readable and lively; but it was not until he began to leave the plane of conscious reason, and had descended into the underworld of his dreams and memories, that he was able to display the full force of his literary gifts. His later poems were composed " *dans un état de rêverie surnaturaliste.*" They cannot be described, on the other hand, as " automatic writing "—the uncensored outpourings of the unconscious mind have seldom any permanent interest; but the processes that produced them were certainly less deliberate than those of almost any other nineteenth-century European writer. They resulted, it might be more accurate to say, from an extremely gradual process of crystallisation, in which successive deposits of thought and feeling were fused, under mental pressure, into a luminous poetic whole. Some of the original deposits can still be uncovered; and a detailed analysis was recently made of the celebrated *El Desdichado*[1] (which proves to include a reflection, subtilised and transfigured, of a lithe young Englishwoman he had once watched swimming in the sea near Naples, who also appears in the sonnet *Delfica*; while Aurélia, or Jenny Colon, is the " *seule ètoilé* " whose extinction had left him widowed and disconsolate) and of *Artémis*, a poem at first sight wrapped in even deeper mystery. Like a modern poet's, Gérard's verses are full of private references: unlike the average contemporary versifier, he is able to give these references a general poetic

---

[1] *Gérard de Nerval* 1808-1855. Poet, Traveller, Dreamer. By S. A. Rhodes. Philosophical Library, New York.

application. The ruined tower, the disconsolate prince, the extinguished star for which *El Desdichado* has assumed perpetual mourning, the siren cleaving her way through the translucent Mediterranean calm, become symbols of a spiritual odyssey in which he persuades us that we have all shared.

Cyril Tourneur

THE sad antithesis of desire and disillusioned satiety, of physical longings and subsequent moral nausea, has been the means of procuring us some of the greatest lyric and dramatic poetry of the modern world. For here was a conflict of which the ancients—if we except certain Latin poets, themselves no doubt influenced by the first uneasy intimations of the Christian spirit—would have understood almost nothing. Relegate the sexual commerce to the category of mere indispensable bodily functions, and the universe you bring into being, though possibly a more rational, is also an emptier and duller, place. Unquestionably, the Elizabethan Age owed a great deal to this strained and artificial opposition, which lent a colouring of the deepest despair to the elementary, unalarming fact illustrated in the "*post coitum tristie*" of a pagan moralist. Half-pagan and half-Christian, an Elizabethan poet knew the pains that belong to both. Was not the Devil sick? And the sickness, that kept him vibrating painfully between moods of extreme lasciviousness and utter abnegation, had its roots not only in maladies of the spirit but in maladies of the body, too. During the opening decades of the sixteenth century, a wave of venereal disease, sweeping its path across Europe, had reached England. In the royal blood of the Tudors the contagion had already done its

25

work. Princes and noblemen, at home and abroad, were willing to pay huge prices for the nostrums of the itinerant specialist; while the terror that the disease inspired, the horror aroused by its variety of atrocious and disgusting symptoms, made " the pox " a never-failing source alike of ribaldry, satire and the weightiest moral argument. In his own individual style, each of the Elizabethan dramatists has reproduced something of the prevailing atmosphere. The villain rants, the clown gibes; noses can scarcely be mentioned, so evocative are those organs of the common, dreadful preoccupation. The characters of the drama seem incessantly to be prying beneath one another's gilded and brocaded harness, scenting out beneath pearl-embroidered velvets and voluminous, all-concealing farthingales, the hideous suppuration of some secret and shameful sore. A curious morbidity results; even the wise and virtuous Prospero, when he warns Ferdinand on no account to anticipate the marriage ceremony, addresses the young Prince in terms of the most appalling harshness, threatening him with offspring hare-lipped and an inheritance of manifold ghastly diseases, and concludes with the gloomy observation that " the strongest oaths are straw to the fire i' the blood." This atmosphere of suspicion and brooding disgust achieves its height of sublimity and rhetorical extravagance in the lust-ridden and blood-stained plays of Cyril Tourneur.

For, in Tourneur's plays, the dramatist, not content with themes of violent melodrama, has imposed upon his characters proper names which can leave us no doubt at all as to what we are to expect from their actions—Lussurioso, Spurio, Ambitioso, Supervacua, Levidulcia, Cataplasma, Soquette and Languebeau Snuffe. Having thus branded them at the outset, Tourneur loses no time in plunging his personages into an ingenious inferno, where assassination and incest shake hands. Consider, for example, the exordium of *The Revenger's Tragedy:*

> *Duke! royal lecher! go, grey-haired adultery!*
> *And thou his son, as impious steeped as he:*
> *And thou his bastard, true begot in evil:*
> *And thou his duchess, that will do with devil:*
> *Four excellent characters!*

This is to out-fulminate Bosola; but then the character of the disappointed underling, criminally embittered and ripe for every mischief, was a general property of the Elizabethan stage. One conjectures, too, that Bosola and his kindred were figures not uncommonly to be met with in the ordinary walks of Elizabethan life. The dramatists themselves, we learn, were sometimes glad enough to lend a hand in the squalid and devious game of Elizabethan political intrigue. There seems, for instance, to be good reason for believing that Marlowe had played the secret agent, and that, when he died, it was not romantically stabbed to death by the " bawdy serving-man " of legend but unobtrusively put out of the way because he knew more than was convenient. Similarly, Cyril Tourneur, if we accept Professor Allardyce Nichol's tentative identification of the dramatist with a Captain William Turnour frequently referred to in the secret correspondence of ministers, emerges as great a ruffian as any, " a man of the most vicious life and habits . . . up to the eyes in evil principles and plans, of a most restless nature," a devotee " of no faith or rather of every faith," " as short of cash as he is of honour." He appears dramatically at Venice, " man of medium stature, dressed in the French fashion, with a French hat, black embroidered with silver. A cloak of grey cloth, lined with velvet of nearly the same colour. Doublet of olive-green English fustian. Hose of French cut. The heels, the turn-over and laces of his boots red." The secretary of the English ambassador is requesting the Council of Ten to have him apprehended. A few weeks later, the ambassador, Sir Henry Wotton, is writing a hasty note to Lord Salisbury, which includes the remark that, as Turnour claimed to have done his Lordship "some notable services," he had decided to intervene to prevent his either being tortured or strangled; and there the matter rests. . . .

Cyril Tourneur himself, supposing Cyril and William, after all, to be not one but two, had led, we are informed, an adventurous and chequered life, and suffered imprisonment for some unknown misdemeanour. Having digested these details and supplied the background of an ill-conditioned and tempestuous existence—the career of a man who was now menial and now confidant, now poet and now spy, who sneaked to and fro upon errands which he dare not divulge, those elegant boots of his, with the red laces and the red turn-over, getting down-at-heel, the silver braid of his hat-band becoming somewhat tarnished, imprisoned in London, jailed at Venice and in great danger of being tortured or strangled or, perhaps, both—how much easier it is, quite apart from the extraordinary force and vividness of the language, to attune our ears to the pitch of his terrific harangue:

> *Faith, if the truth were known, I was begot*
> *After some gluttonous dinner; some stirring dish*
> *Was my first father, when deep healths went round*
> *And ladies' cheeks were painted red with wine,*
> *Their tongues, as short and nimble as their heels,*
> *Uttering sweet words and thick . . .*
> *In such a whispering and withdrawing hour,*
> *When base male-bawds kept sentinel at stair-head,*
> *Was I stol'n softly . . .*

28

Cyril Torneur

Like Bosola, old Gloucester's bastard and a host of others, Spurio is haunted, and his imagination corroded, by the idea of his back-stairs origin and the memory of the clandestine employments with which he has been obliged to soil his hands. Hence the Machiavellian braggadocio so characteristic of the Elizabethan tragic muse:

> *It will confirm me bold—the child o' the court;*
> *Let blushes dwell i' the country. Impudence!*
> *Thou goddess of the palace, mistress of mistresses,*
> *To whom the costly perfumed people pray,*
> *Strike thou my forehead into dauntless marble,*
> *Mine eyes to steady sapphires.*

Is not the voice that speaks there, a reader may be inclined to wonder, the echo of Tourneur's own agonised determination? But Tourneur was a poet, and, as he speaks, the phantasmagoria of experience acquire the gloomy elevation and majestic proportions of some dark, confusing dream which often lapses into sheer nightmare but sometimes rises free of it upon a note of sustained lyrical perplexity:

> *And now methinks I could e'en chide myself*
> *For doating on her beauty, though her death*
> *Shall be revenged after no common action.*
> *Does the silk-worm expend her yellow labours*
> *For thee? For thee does she undo herself?*
> *Are lordships sold to maintain ladyships,*
> *For the poor benefit of a bewildering minute?*

John Ford

AMONG THE mysterious Elizabethans, clustered in varying degrees of inscrutability about the immense Shakespearian enigma, few are more perplexing than a dramatist who was born in 1585 and probably died during the mid-years of the seventeenth century, author of *'Tis Pity She's a Whore* and that even wilder production entitled *The Broken Heart*. We know little of Marlowe, almost nothing that is revelatory of Webster or Cyril Tourneur: the one personal reference to John Ford in Elizabethan literature intensifies the air of strangeness and remoteness with which his dramas are surrounded:

> *Deep in a dump John Forde was alone got,*
> *With folded arms and melancholy hat.*

From this curiously vivid couplet we derive most of our knowledge of the extraordinary anatomist of the passions whose plays appeared during the long twilight of the splendid Elizabethan heyday. We see him shy, gloomy, self-absorbed; we picture him as a character whose imagination revolved with monomaniac zeal round tormenting inward problems. He had none, we deduce, of Shakespeare's openness and sweetness, none of Jonson's common-sense vigour and massive erudition. We may doubt if he was a man of numerous ideas or lively social interests. But certain themes had always fascinated him; and out of those themes —which were almost obsessions—he wove his unequal but, at its occasional best, rare and lasting life-work.

Like Tourneur's, John Ford's was plainly a distempered and discontented spirit; and a recent critic[1] has dealt at considerable length with Ford's debt to the great seventeenth-century treatise on mental distraction, the *Anatomy of Melancholy*. Ford, he is able to show, was deeply versed in Robert Burton's theories and clinical observations. It is possible that he attributes to this relationship too exclusive an importance; for, although every writer tends to fall under the spell of the philosophic and scientific theories current during his period, he is only successful as an artist in so far as he digests and, in the process of digesting, endeavours to transcend them. There is a link between Balzac and Mesmer, between Proust and Bergson; but neither Mesmerism nor the Bergsonian philosophy played a part that was more than incidental in the development of the *Comédie Humaine* and *À la Recherche du Temps Perdu*. That part, nevertheless, we must acknowledge and understand: and it seems evident that Burton's theory of the passions (based on the doctrines of Hippocrates and Galen, with various " accretions from mediæval lore ") gave Ford's individual poetic gifts a stimulus they needed.

That his beliefs now strike us as absurd is obviously beside the point. Once again, the truth that lies in great art shines forth against a dusky background of intellectual error. Ford's psychology (to use the term in its narrower sense) has gone the way of Milton's theology and Dante's cosmology. His tragedies survive on a completely different plane. Yet, as we read them, it is as well to remember that they are the work of a dramatist firmly convinced that the

[1] *The Tragic Music of John Ford*. By G.F. Sensabaugh. Oxford University Press.

body and mind of man were dominated by four " humours "
—blood, phlegm, choler, melancholy—which controlled the
physical organism, and by " spirits " which were " expressed
from the blood " and acted as mediators between the mind
and body; and that the human *ego* was the victim—often
the helpless victim—of the dispositions they engendered.
Thus Ford, though a surprisingly " modern " writer in
some respects, in other and less important respects seems
decidedly archaic. Havelock Ellis has compared him to
Flaubert and Stendhal—a comparison of scanty critical
service, which, could he overhear it from beyond the grave,
might cause the peculiar outline of Ford's hat to assume a
yet more melancholy indentation. No, the poet was
essentially a man of his period, steeped in its theories, his
mind conditioned by its atmosphere. It is not the rightness
or wrongness of an artist's beliefs, but the imaginative use
to which he puts them, that concerns the critic of a later
age who attempts to estimate his genius.

There can be no doubt that the use Ford made of
Burton's fantastic hypothesis was splendid and effective. It
strengthened his natural fatalism and coloured his gloomy
preoccupation with the tragedies of the human heart. And
here the question arises, why the dramatists of the Elizabethan and Jacobean era were so stimulated by the con-
sideration of a certain type of heartbreak: whence sprang
the mood of black pessimism latent in most Elizabethan
poetry. Perhaps it was the conflict between the old and the
new worlds that puzzled and dismayed them—between
a mediæval hatred of the flesh and the exquisite appre-
hension of physical beauty they had caught from the
Renaissance. Nor (as I have suggested when writing of
Tourneur) can we discount an historical accident—the
appalling spread of syphilis, which attacked and killed or
cruelly disfigured almost overnight. " Wit with his wanton-

ness tasted death's bitterness; Hell's executioner had no ears for to hear what vain art could reply." Behind the espaliered garden-wall a heavy bell was tolling. Fear gave lust a sharper edge: pleasure got an added relish from the phantoms of jealousy and the shadow of separation: images of desire and visionary purity struggled together for possession of the tormented lover's spirit.

Men of the Renaissance brought to this inward struggle little of the defensive equipment, of the intellectual armour-plating, that it demanded. Allowing for a few magnificent exceptions, they had more energy than poise, great pene-trative and intuitive powers, qualified by the narrowness they owed to a civilisation as yet narrow and fragmentary. They had the impetuosity and charm of youth, and much of youth's unsteadiness. Ford inherited a touch of the Eliza-bethan fire, and not a few of the accompanying faults and crudities. His view of life was intense, but it was also extremely limited. His central characters are usually maniacs: they rarely develop but go rushing madly forward. We find nothing of that tolerance, half-pitiful, half-cynical, which shines over the troubled surface of Shakespeare's darkest tragedies. True to what his editor has called Burton's " deterministic " doctrine, he depicts his personages as the sport, helpless and foredoomed, of their own atrocious passions.

To re-read Ford is an exciting, but slightly exhausting, task. His work allows no relief: here is no kindly play of half-tones, no respite from the burden of feeling, none of the fantasy, the delight in wit for its own sake, that soften the tragic eloquence of the equally pessimistic Webster. Ford's comic interludes are weak and per-functory: when he digresses from his main theme, he is often dull and heavy-handed: he achieves his greatest triumphs by driving straight ahead. Take *'Tis Pity She's a*

Whore, a tragedy concerned with the incestuous love of a young man for his sister. When the play opens, we are at once presented with Giovanni, attempting by ingenious, sophistical arguments to justify the consummation of his love, which he feels to be predestined. He accomplishes his object at the expense of reason, peace and modesty. We observe the happiness of the two lovers—a happiness so complete that their guilty pastime itself seems strangely beautifully innocent. Then the world closes in upon them. Annabella is forced into a wretched marriage: her husband enters a hell of jealousy, from which he emerges in the guise of a revengeful tyrant. There is a last solemn, pathetic scene, with " *Annabella* richly dressed and *Giovanni* discovered lying on a bed." Annabella, not Giovanni, speaks of their approaching doom:

> *Be not deceived, my brother;*
> *This banquet is an harbinger of death*
> *To you and me; resolve yourself it is,*
> *And be prepared to welcome it.*

GIO: *Well, then;*
> *The schoolmen teach that all this globe of earth*
> *Shall be consumed to ashes in a minute.*

ANN: *So I have read, too.*

GIO: *But 'twere somewhat strange*
> *To see the waters burn: could I believe*
> *This might be true, I could believe as well*
> *There might be hell or heaven.*

ANN: *That's most certain.*

GIO: *A dream, a dream! else in this other world*
> *We should know one another.*

ANN: *So we shall.*

GIO: *Have you heard so?*

ANN: *For certain.*

34

John Ford

Gio: *But d'ye think*
That I shall see you there? You look on me?
May we kiss one another, prate or laugh,
Or do as we do here?

Meanwhile, Giovanni's desperate resolution—to kill his
sister and then himself—is slowly gaining ground:

Kiss me. If ever after-times should hear
Of our fast-knit affections, though perhaps
The laws of conscience and of civil use
May justly blame us, yet when they but know
Our loves, that love will wipe away that rigour
Which would in other incests be abhorred.
Give me your hand: how sweetly life doth run
In these well-coloured veins! how constantly
These palms do promise health! but I could chide
With Nature for this cunning flattery.
Kiss me again—forgive me.

Lamb's criticism of Ford (though he found in the
tragedies abundant material for moral reprobation) seems
the most acute and sympathetic that has yet been published.
He notices the plainness and linear severity of Ford's
dramatic method, observing that the poet " sought for
sublimity, not by parcels in metaphors or visible images, but
directly where she has her full residence in the heart of man;
in the actions and sufferings of the greatest minds. There
is a grandeur of the soul above mountains, seas, and the
elements. Even in the poor perverted reason of Giovanni
and Annabella we discover traces of that fiery particle, which,
in the irregular starting from out of the road of beaten
action, discovers something of a right line even in
obliquity. . . ." Lamb concludes that " Ford was of the
first order of poets." This conclusion may impress us as

far-fetched. It is true, however, that, both in *The Broken Heart* and in *'Tis Pity She's a Whore* (as in Heywood's brilliant domestic tragedy, *A Woman Killed by Kindness*), the genius of the English drama appears to be reaching out towards new fields and, by discarding the elaborate conceits and euphuistic imagery of the Elizabethan poets, seeking to find a mode more in accordance with the spirit of the period, with the taste of a century in which, " Natural Science " had begun to spread its wings. That development was cut short by the rank growth of English puritanism and by the outbreak of the Civil War. *'Tis Pity She's a Whore* and *The Broken Heart* were printed in 1633: Prynne's furious *Histrio-Mastix* had appeared a year earlier. By 1641 actors were already lamenting their " sad and solitary conditions." The first shots were fired in 1642, and an ordinance of the Lords and Commons commanded that, " while these sad causes and set-times of humiliation do continue, public stage plays shall cease and be forborne." So Ford stands, not at the opening of a new and fruitful epoch, but at the termination of a literary period that had spent its youth and gusto. With dejected hat and pensively folded arms, he lingers on in a dark corner of English dramatic history, unapproachable, disconsolate, now casting an abstracted glance at the flamelit tormented figures who writhe and weep around him—Giovanni, Annabella, Soranzo, Bassanes, Penthea—now listening to the faint echoes of an old, unhappy past:

> *Parthenophil is lost, and I would see him;*
> *For he is like to something I remember,*
> *A great while since, a long, long time ago.*

Philip Massinger

DURING THE first half of the nineteenth century, the English theatre would appear to have been more genuinely and broadly democratic than at any other period. " Give me the days when I played to the pit," the veteran actor Charles Mathews used to exclaim. " The stalls are profitable, but the pit was pulsating! " Edmund Kean was of the same persuasion; and one night when he returned home from Drury Lane, where he had triumphed in the part of Massinger's Sir Giles Overreach, and Mrs. Kean asked apprehensively what Lord Essex, a prominent member of the Drury Lane Committee, had had to say about his acting, " Damn Lord Essex! " Kean retorted. " The *pit* rose at me." A melodramatic *tour de force*, calculated to appeal to the most proletarian sections of his enthusiastic and appreciative, but not too sensitive audience, Kean's presentation of Overreach made an equally deep impression upon the whole theatre. Hazlitt praised it at length: many years later Byron recollected the gesture of frantic contempt with which Overreach spat at Lovell. His performance has been described again and again, and was painted by George Clint in a picture which to-day hangs in the Garrick Club. It was terrifying, chilling, electric; and, while the ladies who crowded the boxes were frightened into fainting fits and " carried out screaming," and the author of *Childe Harold*—

37

on somewhat poor authority—was reported to have succumbed to a strong convulsive seizure, Kean's fellow-actors at the end of the drama were themselves completely pulverised, Mrs. Glover (we learn from Kean's biographer, F. W. Hawkins) "fainted outright on the stage, Mrs. Horn staggered to a chair and wept aloud at the appalling sight, and Munden . . . stood so transfixed with astonishment and terror that he was taken off by the armpits, his legs trailing and his eyes riveted with a species of fascination on Kean's convulsed and blackened countenance."

Such was the climax of the play, when Overreach, that "cruel extortioner," baffled in all his designs, encircled by his enemies, an assemblage of crafty but sanctimonious Jacobean lay-figures, explodes in a final burst of fury and vituperation. Tearing open his shirt-collar, Kean is said to have rent the stuff to ribbons, "with face lurid, eyes distended, lips swollen and parted at the corners, teeth set and visage quivering." Were Massinger's play devoid of literary merit, we should still be curious to know something of this so-called "*Comoedie*" from which the greatest of English tragic actors evoked what was once described as "the most terrific exhibition of human passion . . . witnessed on the modern stage." In fact, *A New Way to Pay Old Debts*, which Massinger wrote for the Queen's Men "probably between July and December 1625," and of which the first and only Quarto was published in 1633, is a production that on its own account deserves sympathetic reading. Kean was Overreach's finest interpreter; but the play remained a popular stock piece until the close of the Victorian Age, and proved even more successful in America than in England. Nor are its dramatic qualities difficult to discern. It moves fast: it has a sufficiently exciting plot: it displays—or it purports to display—the advantages of virtue and the inevitable fate of wickedness. Above all, the dramatist's dialogue is supremely smooth and fluent. No Shakespearian sublimity here, none of the astonishing flashes of a Webster or a Tourneur; at the same time there is none of the literary conceits, none of the learnedly elaborate curled and, spangled euphuisms, which puzzle the average modern playgoer as much as they delighted and entertained his Elizabethan counterpart.

Massinger's verse is often admirable prose; but of his " excellent metre " Coleridge declared that it was " a better model for dramatists in general to imitate than Shake-spear's," since it was " the nearest approach to the language of real life at all compatible with a fixed metre. In Massinger, as in all our poets before Dryden, in order to make har-monious verse in the reading it is absolutely necessary that the meaning should be understood: when the meaning is once seen, the harmony is perfect. . . ." Massinger's meaning is usually plain enough—too plain perhaps for the literary critic who puts subtlety of presentation before energy of handling. His sense of drama clung to the surface of life, rarely involving itself in profound emotional issues, with the result that his personages' adventures and misadventures are apt, now and then, to seem strangely insignificant, and that when a hero is betrayed and ruined, or a virtuous character injured and insulted, " it is the same (Coleridge has pointed out) as if any other accident of nature had occurred, a pig run under his legs, or his horse had thrown him. There is no dramatic art in it."

Possibly his age was at fault. Son of a Steward of the Household to the second Earl of Pembroke, Philip Massinger was born at Salisbury in 1583 or 1584, and no doubt was brought up at Wilton among reminders of some of the brightest and kindliest figures of the Elizabethan heyday. He was described in the baptismal register as " *generosus* " or of gentle birth; but evidently his fortune was meagre,

39

or his personal life extravagant; and from leaving Oxford in 1606 until his death in 1640 he earned his bread as a sweated dramatist about the London play-houses. Wilton belonged to a romantic past: the Jacobean present was less kindly and less stimulating. A new plutocracy had begun to emerge; and the character of Sir Giles Overreach is thought to have been founded on that of Sir Giles Mompesson, a creature of the royal favourite, George Villiers, Duke of Buckingham. Mompesson, whose malpractices, connected with the recent licensing commission for inns, created universal uproar, had been disgraced and banished the kingdom only a few years earlier; and Overreach is the type of seventeenth-century *parvenu*, insolent and proud and unashamed, gnawing away at the estates of his aristocratic neighbours, who, temporarily worsted and baffled, in the end turn upon him and by superior craft destroy him. Overreach defies them in a wild paroxysm of unrepentant anger. He is removed, struggling and fulminating, to the chains and straw of Bedlam.

Seldom has literary turpitude been so entirely unrelieved; yet such genius as Massinger possessed was concentrated upon Overreach, whose stature increases as the drama proceeds, while his self-righteous accusers shrink to the dimensions of noisy and abusive puppets. Arrayed against him is an oddly assorted crew—the Lady Allworth, a rich and virtuous widow, Young Allworth, her stepson and gentleman page to Lord Lovell, Lord Lovell, a retired soldier, and Wellborn, a patrician rake, ruined by his dissipations. When the play opens, with a characteristic swing, poor Wellborn is being refused credit outside a squalid alehouse:

WELLBORN: *No bouze? nor no Tobacco?*
TAPWELL: *Not a suck Sir,*

40

> *Nor the remainder of a single can*
> *Left by a drunken porter, all night pall'd too.*

FROTH: *Not the dropping at the tap for your morning's*
> *draught, Sir,*
> *'Tis verity I assure you.*

Wellborn's plight is indeed pathetic; but, if the play can be said to possess a moral, it concerns the admirable solidarity of the English upper classes. Wellborn has declined and degenerated, apparently beyond repair; his habits are deplorable; his suit is old and filthy; he carries a cudgel instead of a sword. Yet, as soon as it is a question of the dissolute but well-born Wellborn *versus* the sound and prosperous, yet newly knighted, Overreach even the squeamish Lady Allworth is prepared to sink her prejudices. Together, Allworth, Wellborn and Lovell attack the *parvenu's* snobbery. He wishes his daughter Margaret to marry a nobleman, whereas Margaret (a hateful and hypocritical girl) wishes to marry young Tom Allworth; and Lovell, her pretended suitor, lends himself to the plot with unremitting diligence. Overreach is thoroughly cozened and deluded. Virtue prevails; and the resourceful landed gentry quit the stage exultant.

Yet it is Overreach who holds our attention and, to a point, commands our sympathy. Although in one respect he is scarcely more individual than Marrall, Tapwell, Froth or Mr. Justice Greedy (a cormorant magistrate perpetually lusting after Overreach's banquets), Massinger is able to confer on him an air of genuine magnitude. He is the Superman, the supreme egotist:

> *Why is not the whole world (he rages)*
> *Included in myself?*

—a man of unbreakable courage, whose fury leaves his

antagonists, even the soldierly Lovell, trembling and sweating:

> *He's gone, I wonder how the Earth can bear*
> *Such a portent! I, that have lived a Soldier . . .*
> *To hear this blasphemous beast, am bathed all over*
> *In a cold sweat: yet like a mountain he . . .*
> *Is not more shaken, than Olympus is*

—a being of instinctive ferocity, who advises his daughter to permit seduction, but vows that he will wade through blood if her seducer does not marry her:

> *How? forsake thee?*
> *Do I wear a sword for fashion? or is this arm*
> *Shrunk? or withered? does there live a man*
> *Of that large list I have encountered with*
> *Can truly say I ere gave inch of ground . . . ?*

He is at his noblest when his grandeur is on the verge of toppling; and then Kean, astride Overreach, climbed to heights of tragedy:

> LOVELL: *Are you not frightened with the imprecations,*
> *And curses, of whole families made*
> *wretched . . . ?*
> OVERREACH: *Yes, as rocks are*
> *When foamy billows split themselves against*
> *Their flinty ribs; or as the Moon is moved,*
> *When wolves, with hunger pined, howl at her*
> *brightness.*

Efficient rhetoric, one might have considered; but luckily there is a contemporary account of how Kean contrived to extract from the lines their quintessential poetic value. " I seem still to hear the words (wrote Doran) and the voice as I pen this passage; now composed, now grand as the foamy

billows; so flutelike on the word ' moon,' creating a scene
with the sound and anon sharp, harsh, fierce in the last line,
with a look upward from those matchless eyes, that rendered
the troop visible, and their howl perceptible to the ear; the
whole serenity of the man, and the solidity of his temper,
being less illustrated by the assurance in the succeeding
words than by the exquisite music in the tone with which
he uttered the word ' brightness.' " Edmund Kean has
vanished into the limbo of dead actors; *A New Way to
Pay Old Debts* is a play that still re-enacts itself in the
theatre of the reader's mind.

Lord Hervey

" How GREAT a Change has been wrought in Female
Manners within these few Years in England! (remarked
Mrs. Thrale from Brighton on November 4th, 1782). I
was reading the Letter in the 3d. Vol. of the Spectator 217,
where the Man complains of his indelicate Mistress: I
read it aloud to my little daughters of 11 and 12 Years old,
and even the Maid who was dressing my hair, burst out
o'laughing at the Idea of *a Lady* saying her Stomach ach'd,
or that something stuck between her Teeth. Sure if our
Morals are as much mended as our Manners, we are grown
a most virtuous Nation! " Mrs. Thrale was an intelligent
social critic; but not only female manners suffered an
immense change during her long lifetime. The revolution
was far more profound, and affected every sphere of life, so
that the Age of Adam considered the Age of Kent a remote
and slightly barbarous period, in which furniture was heavy
and speech was rude, and the English character, exemplified
by such sensual giants as Sir Robert Walpole, retained
much of its primitive strength together with a large ad-
mixture of its native coarseness. The distinction, however,
is not always made by modern students of the eighteenth
century. They fail to observe how real was the development
that had occurred between 1730, say, and 1760 or 1770,
and how numerous and striking were the reforms on which

the contemporaries of Mrs. Thrale felt that they could pride themselves. " Elegance," " refinement," " modesty," " sensibility " were words particularly dear to late-eighteenth century commentators; and everywhere they saw proofs of the rapid advance of civilisation. Men and women who were painted by Reynolds and Gainsborough—pensive, reflective, gently amused, in surroundings that combined a hint of grandeur with an ingenious suggestion of graceful informality—gazed in astonishment at the family portraits of their immediate forebears, those wasp-waisted wooden-faced dolls representing dignitaries and maids of honour at the court of George II, when Bellenden was a reigning beauty and Hervey a fashionable wit.

Just as portrait-painters tell us little of the age, so the written memorials of the early-Georgian epoch are strangely unrevealing. Hervey stands almost alone, exceptional in his gifts, yet highly characteristic of the social period he sprang from. It was an age of contrasts—and few men have had more contrasting attributes: a period of cruelty and corruption—and Hervey was as cruel as a cat, and disdained the affectation of morality either in his personal or in his political life. He was a trifler, an elegant amateur; but he possessed remarkable strength of will and literary ability that would have done a professional writer lasting credit. An invalid of Herculean vitality, he selected and clung to the type of career that he professed to find most wearisome. He pretended to despise his fellow courtiers, and never tired of deriding the arrogance and dullness of his royal patrons; but his days and nights were passed upon the courtly tread-mill, " making a leg " at the appearance of royalty, smiling, flattering, gossiping, with rarely a moment to enjoy as he pleased; the only solitude he could always command, the guarded privacy of his own spirit.

A wily, polished, deliberately elusive personage, Hervey

had been exceedingly handsome in youth; and, though he wooed and wedded the beautiful Molly Lepell, to whom in the intervals of pleasure and business he gave as many as eight children, and was known to have had an amorous intrigue with one at least of Queen Caroline's attractive and ill-conducted maids of honour, his reputation for sexual perversity was never wholly shaken off. Pope sprang on it greedily and gladly. The courtier was involved in the poet's quarrel with Lady Mary Wortley Montagu; and, while Lady Mary was lampooned as " Sappho "—a sluttish she-rake, whose hatred was as venomous as her love was dangerous—Hervey became " Lord Fanny " and then, after he had attempted to retaliate, reappeared as " Sporus."

Not until the first appearance of his *Memoirs*, edited by Croker, in 1848, was it possible to disassociate Hervey from Pope's resounding diatribe. The satire had contained a measure of truth—the subject's character certainly included many odious qualities; but it left out of account a considerable array of complementary virtues. Though Hervey could be cold and cruel, though he was malicious and self-interested and, in his lust for political power, ready to sacrifice both decency and dignity, he was capable of genuine devotion towards the rare human beings whom he loved and trusted. He loved the Queen, as his letters and memoirs show; and he had a passionate, if ambiguous, affection for his friends Henry and Stephen Fox, elevated to the peerage in later life as, respectively, Lord Holland and Lord Ilchester. On their side, at all events, the friendship that sprang up would seem to have been entirely innocent. No doubt they were charmed by so brilliant a worshipper, and delighted to receive the voluminous and informative letters that, evening after evening, he scribbled from St. James's Palace, writing very often on the corner of a card-table, while the King played " commerce and backgammon, and the

Queen at quadrille," the Duke of Grafton took " his nightly opiate of lottery " and slumbered " as usual between the Princesses Amelie and Caroline," and Lord Grantham strolled distractedly from one room to another, bestirring himself " as people stir a fire not with any design . . . but in hopes to make it burn a little brisker, which His Lordship constantly does to no purpose, and yet tries it as constantly as if it had ever once succeeded." For Henry and Stephen Fox, who spent much of their time at their country house in Somerset, surrounded (as Hervey frequently complained) by " those demi-human, demi-brutal boobys, your country neighbours," the friendship of so talented a court-chronicler was a fascinating acquisition. But perhaps they failed to grasp the complexity of the emotions beneath which their friend was labouring.

The story of this unequal intimacy, which Mr. Romney Sedgwick discussed at length in his preface to the *Memoirs*, has been retold in an edition of Hervey's correspondence, compiled by the present Lord Ilchester from a mass of letters and copies of letters, preserved at Ickworth, Melbury and Holland House.[1] He has made, he informs us, numerous deletions, removing passages that in his judgment were definitely " unprintable " and others that he felt to be tedious or repetitive. He also suppressed " a number of long declarations of friendship for the Fox brothers, and of even more sloppy sentiment. . . ." But were the deletions indicated above advisable or really necessary? There is no disguising the fact that Hervey's composition had a definitely homosexual strain, and that, far from concealing his tendencies, he was apt to underline them. Thus to Stephen Fox (whose charm presently prevailed over the attraction of his younger brother) he writes in August, 1851, when he himself was a man of thirty-five and Fox was

[1] *Lord Hervey and His Friends.* Edited by the Earl of Ilchester. Murray.

twenty-seven, that, on hearing Stephen's health proposed at dinner, " I assure you I coloured, and felt just as I imagine your favourite mistress would have done upon the same occasion." And a couple of sentences earlier: " It is unimaginable how many thousand nameless accidents and indescribable sensations prove to me every day how much I am engrossed by one thing." His communications were usually love-letters: and love-letters, shorn of their amatory content, have a somewhat awkward and impoverished air.

Hervey's correspondence, nevertheless, makes an informative and entertaining volume; for, apart from its psychological interest (which might have held the attention of Marcel Proust), it contains illuminating reflections of the social and political background. Hervey was a henchman of Walpole, who in his management of the King through the Queen repeatedly made use of Queen Caroline's subtle favourite; and here is a glimpse of Sir Robert at Houghton, " up to the chin in beef, venison, geese, turkeys, etc.; and generally over the chin in claret, strong beer and punch." Here, too, is a sketch of another confederate, Chesterfield:

He was incessantly entertaining; and though naturally I know your taste is not turned to romances . . . yet the historical, political, amorous, familiar, foreign and domestic novels which he told, were related in so compendious a manner and so lively a style, that I am sure you would have been infinitely pleased . . . I always listen to him as I read poetry, without hoping for a word of truth. . . . If ever I do think of it upon that foot, it is only to admire the fertility of his imagination and the luxuriancy of his invention; and, as one values other people in proportion to their adherence to truth, one admires him most when he deviates most from it. With all this he is positively no liar. . . . His Lordship never thinks of the things he tells being either true or false, and as for deceiving you, provided he is sure you like his manner of telling them, he concerns himself no more about the credit you give to his narrative than he does about the authority he has for them.

We catch echoes of Hervey's furious and rather mysterious quarrel with the unfortunate Frederick Prince of Wales; and we read numerous and glowing tributes to Frederick's profoundly cynical and highly gifted mother. At the outset Hervey's attachment to Caroline may have had a selfish basis; but, as he studied and came to know the Queen, self-interest merged into loyalty, and loyalty into deep affection. Caroline's death, which occurred after appalling agonies in November, 1737, struck him a disastrous blow. Walpole who, during the Queen's agony, had paced his room in desperation, exclaiming " My God, My God, why hast Thou forsaken me? ", was consoled as soon as he discovered that he could govern the King without the Queen's help. But Hervey was made of more sensitive stuff; and, having lost the only woman whom he genuinely admired and loved—towards Lady Hervey his attitude, after the ardours of courtship, was never more than distinctly well-bred—he could not escape from the gathering shadows that fell across his private life. The flippancy and gaiety subsided: melancholy clogged his pen. " Upon my word (he wrote to Count Algarotti) she was a thorough great, wise, good and agreeable woman." And to the Foxes' sister, Mrs. Digby:

I myself who knew her well, who knew her temper, her strength and greatness of mind, her patience, her resignation, her mildness and her indifference to life, could yet have had no conception of her firmness in bodily pain. . . . Let those who used to call her affability falseness, to say her piety was grimace, and her easiness in all situations put on, now blush . . . for all their rancorous insinuations . . . on the best and greatest, not only woman, but human creature that ever was created.

The letters ceased in 1738; but Hervey survived until 1743. Emaciated, pallid but heavily made up—" a painted face and not a tooth in his head! " proclaimed the savage old Duchess of Marlborough, whom Hervey himself at happier moments had so often caricatured—he still hungered after the " shew-bread of Counsel " which he had once eaten with the " Cabinet-priests " in the " Sanctum Sanctorum of politics." But Walpole had fallen from power; and Walpole's successors had no use for the tarnished confidant of the late Queen. He died embittered and disabused, remarking that the " last stages of an infirm life are filthy roads," and that " the further one goes from the capital the more tedious the miles grow." A new generation began to forget him: Thackeray in the *Four Georges* held him up as a subject for journalistic ridicule. Yet his career had its justification, though his ambition had been denied its reward. His *Memoirs*, to which his correspondence provides an extremely useful supplement, entitle him to an honourable niche in the extensive, various and distinguished array of eighteenth-century prose-writers.

MRS THRALE
by George Dance, 1793

Mrs Thrale

THE EIGHTEENTH century was the great age of the English conversation picture: and something of the same homely vividness and bright minuteness, the same care for detail and regard for background, is to be distinguished in the letters and diaries of that delightful period. Here, as in a family group by Copley or Zoffany, is all the ordered diversity and emotional variety of a civilised social life; and, in the midst of such a group, stands Hester Lynch Thrale, the woman of whom Samuel Johnson wrote that he counted the friendship she and her household showed him among the major felicities of a troubled existence; and, again, that she was his " *Thralia dulcis* " and had " a temper the most delightful of any woman I ever knew."

In any account of Mrs. Thrale, the story of her relations with Johnson must form the central episode; and the problem round which it revolves is an old and complex one, based on the very nature of love itself and on the difficulty of effecting a compromise between love and friendship. Whereas friendship is doubly precious if it partakes of love, in the love that wears a colouring of friendship there lurk peculiar dangers. Mrs. Thrale was a woman capable of inspiring deep love, but to whom the experience of loving came late and oddly. She was not beautiful, though by the buxom and high-coloured standards of the age in which she lived she was generally esteemed not unattractive; but she had infinite vivacity and warm affections, a sharp dashing tongue and a brisk intelligence. Staunch, energetic, personally courageous, she possessed an overwhelming, disarming feminity, beside which younger and prettier companions looked pale and characterless. Johnson needed women—both socially and sentimentally. Their society helped to relieve his habitual gloom; and never had his need been more desperate than in 1765, a year that marked one of those mysterious crises which occur in every human life, when the burden of daily existence seems suddenly to become intolerable, and each separate faculty of body and soul appears on the point of turning traitor. He dreaded death, expected damnation and could not contrive to rid himself of a corroding sense of sin. Madness, which he had always feared, might now at length have swallowed him up, had not Arthur Murphy, an old and devoted friend, conceived the excellent plan of carrying him off to dine at Streatham, where he soon recognised the emotional refuge after which his spirit hankered.

Johnson's domestication at Streatham and Southwark first took effect during the summer and autumn months of 1766, and lasted without interruption till 1782. To both parties the arrangement brought many obvious benefits. Mrs. Thrale, when she captured Johnson, had been married three years. Her husband's boon-companions, except for Arthur Murphy, were not amusing; and he himself was neither demonstrative nor very brilliant. Suddenly into the monotonous round of bearing, nursing and frequently losing children, shouldered the vast tormented figure of a man of genius. Only Mrs. Thrale had the power to calm him—she and the atmosphere she radiated and the life at her country house, so variegated yet so pleasant, so smooth but lively. Streatham was his true home; at rest among the

Thrales he had rediscovered the heart's affections. If time could have stood still at 1766, and the summer of his mistress's friendship have proved eternal, Johnson might have died comparatively a happy man.

It is the egotism of love to wish to hold back the clock, or to expect to regulate the beloved's growth according to our own requirements. Mrs. Thrale's character was already formed when she encountered Johnson; and, granted the considerable difference between their ages and the strong claims made by her effusive and emotional temperament, it was inevitable that, as they grew older, they should grow apart. From childhood she had been high-spirited, impetuous, headstrong. The little girl who, during the absence of her scapegrace father, had sat talking to the old coachman, " kicking my Heels on a Corn Binn," and terrified her anxious mother and devoted aunt by showing them how Grandmamma's " four great ramping War-horses; *chevaux entiers* for her carriage, with immense long Manes & Tails . . . would lick my hand for a lump of sugar or fine white bread," had developed into a combination of successful wife, hard-worked business-woman, diarist, salon-keeper and dazzling social chatter-box who stormed and reduced the London citadel of the exclusive " Blues."

One need, however—one ambition perhaps—had not yet been satisfied. Johnson might be genuinely in love with Mrs. Thrale (though his admiration was consistent with complete propriety), but Mrs. Thrale had never experienced a real emotional weakness. Her marriage had been a matter of common sense and always remained so. It is clear that the brewer of Southwark must have had solid qualities, since he commanded the respect, and could compel the silence, of Dr. Johnson—" There, there (he would remark firmly), now we have had enough for one lecture . . . we will not be upon education any more till after dinner, if you

please "; but as a husband he was equally prolific and
unfaithful, a silent, phlegmatic, greedy personage with
numerous double chins. The children who survived took
after their father—they were not expansive. Queeney, in
particular, was obstinate to an " uncommon Degree ";
" her Discretion (noted Mrs. Thrale) is beyond her years."
Harry, the heir—a delightful enthusiast—had died in
childhood; and, with his death, her husband slid slowly
downhill into gluttonous lethargy. She was proud of her
daughters, those graceful and accomplished girls. But they
had disappointed her while they were children; and they
grew up to snub her. Whatever faults Queeney might
possess (recorded Mrs. Thrale with a mixture of satisfaction
and exasperation) they were certainly " not my faults, of
Confidence, Loquacity and foolish Sensibility." A moment
would arrive when the " foolish sensibility " that had long
been confined to ordinary social intercourse and to the
endearing epithets that she was apt to bestow upon all her
friends—" Dear Dr. Johnson," " Poor Dear Dr. Burney,"
" Poor Pretty Siddons "—suddenly burst its bounds and
flooded her personal life.

Meanwhile, few of her associates seem to have suspected
that Mrs. Thrale had literary talent. Mr. Thrale, however,
was less undiscerning; and in 1776, a few weeks before the
thirteenth anniversary of their marriage, he presented his
wife with a solidly bound set of quarto manuscript books.
There were six of them in all, and on its cover of undressed
calf each bore a red label stamped in gold with a single word:
Thraliana. Thus did the slothful and self-indulgent brewer
of Streatham pay an unexpected tribute to his wife's
intelligence; and seldom has a gift been better or more
promptly used. Remembering the good advice she had
once received from Dr. Johnson, Mrs. Thrale proceeded
to pour into these volumes every anecdote that struck her

and every scrap of talk she thought worthy of recollection, together with *memorabilia* of passing interest as they happened to accumulate in her lively, untidy head. The result was an odd combination of anecdotage and autobiography, a collection of material both trumpery and precious, only to be compared to the contents of some old-fashioned workbox where trinkets of gold and silver lie mixed up with screws of yellowed paper bearing scribbled recipes, twists of silk, ancient *bouts rimés* and fragments of tarnished brocade.

Yet from this engaging muddle how clearly emerges the character of the woman whose existence it reflects! Irrepressible while she lived, Mrs. Thrale after death has refused to be extinguished. No longer can we regard her merely as Johnson's " dearest mistress," a personage of secondary importance, privileged to play a part in the career of a great and unhappy man. Her rehabilitation is now complete. Knowing her as well as we have come to do, we are bound to admit that in her own right and by virtue of her own personal attainments, no less than as a friend of a man of genius, she merits our attention and demands our sympathy. Her good qualities were numerous—courage, independence, a disposition to be pleased and a desire to please in turn. Her faults (as she herself honestly agreed) included over-enthusiasm, talkativeness and a certain vein of emotional silliness. Both aspects of her temperament are mirrored in the pages of *Thraliana*,[1] a book that, although it may be far too voluminous, too crowded here and there with insignificant jottings, has at length taken the place it deserves among genuine literary self-portraits.

Not that Mrs. Thrale was a self-analyst in the ordinary sense of the term. When she looked into her glass—which

[1] *Thraliana: The Diary of Mrs. Hester Lynch Thrale* (later Mrs. Piozzi), 1776-1809. Edited by Katharine C. Balderston. Oxford: Clarendon Press.

she did figuratively from time to time, and literally (one
suspects) at frequent intervals—it was without the splenetic
anxiety of the habitual self-appraiser, but with a certain
mingling of tolerance, humour, honesty and positive
affection. Considering all things, she seems to assure herself
—Thrale's dullness and selfishness, Johnson's possessiveness, the difficulty of bearing and rearing children, the
shocks, disappointments, *ennuis*, to which in the natural
course of existence one was continually exposed—she had
really very little to be ashamed of and some reason to feel
satisfied with the image she found there. She might not be
able to hold her tongue, but she could keep her counsel.
Was it not Mrs. Thrale whom Dr. Johnson had made the
confidante of the " Secret far dearer to him than Life "?
Did her friends not crowd around her in bewildering variety
—from Johnson, Burke, Reynolds, Goldsmith to Miss
Sophia Streatfield (the " beautiful S. S.," adored by Thrale),
who combined a knowledge of Greek with a reputation for
crying more prettily than any other woman, and who sometimes obliged the company by weeping for their benefit?
If the hospitality of Streatham was magnificent and the
gatherings there distinguished, Mrs. Thrale could claim
that its social structure was of her own creation.

Her beginnings, after all, had been far from brilliant.
Not the least interesting section of *Thraliana* is an autobiographical sketch (hitherto unpublished in full) which tells
the story of her childhood, education and early married life.
Mr. Thrale was not the man to inspire passion in an
inexperienced yet highly strung girl. Their union from the
outset had been a *mariage de raison*; but Mrs. Thrale even
at that period was of a philosophic turn—" My mother lived
with me (she records quietly) & I was content; I re'd to
her in the Morning, played Back Gammon with her at
Noon, & worked Carpets with her in the Evening." And it

was not until she had been married some years, and borne
several children, that Johnson had opened her eyes to the
insignificance of the life she led:

> One Day that I mentioned Mr. Thrale's cold Carriage
> to me, tho' with no Resentment, for it occasioned in me
> no Dislike; He said in Reply—Why how for Heaven's
> Sake Dearest Madam should any Man delight in a Wife
> that is to him neither Use nor Ornament? He cannot
> talk to you about his Business, which you do not under-
> stand; nor about his Pleasures which you do not partake;
> if you have Wit or Beauty you shew them nowhere, so he
> has none of the Reputation; if you have Economy or
> Understanding you employ neither in Attention to his
> Property. You divide your Time between your Mamma
> & your Babies, & wonder you do not by that means
> become agreeable to your Husband. This was so plain
> I could not fail to comprehend it, & gently hinted to my
> Mother I had some Curiosity about the Trade. . . .

Mrs. Salusbury, who was exceedingly jealous of Johnson's
influence, opposed any plan for her daughter's emancipation; and while she lived (writes Mrs. Thrale) " I went on
in the old Way, brought a Baby once a Year, lost some of
them & grew so anxious about the rest, that I now fairly
cared for nothing else, but them & her; & not a little for
Johnson, who I felt to be my true Friend, though I could
not break thro' my Chains to take his Advice. . . ." But
within the chrysalis of domesticity the strong-minded
business-woman and talkative *bas bleu* was waiting to
emerge.

Thraliana gives an impression of the change that followed.
It shows the multitude of her interests, the restless energy
with which she flung herself into every department of a busy
and exhausting career, the quickness of her wit, and the

sharpness of her observation. It is not, however, by any means a continuous chronicle of Mrs. Thrale's progress. From volume to volume, and year to year, the method varies; and, whereas the first volume is a rag-bag of miscellaneous anecdotes, the opening ninety-seven pages of the second are devoted to a record of Johnson's talk; while half-way through the third, under pressure of the misfortunes and anxieties by which she was suddenly attacked, at the time of her husband's death and her own re-marriage, she began to keep an intermittent private diary. Naturally, it is the section of Johnsoniana that proves to be of most immediate literary value. Yet they form, comparatively speaking, only a very small part of this massive compilation, just as Johnson himself (decisive as was his rôle in Mrs. Thrale's development) occupied only two decades of her long, overcrowded, intensely exciting life. Johnson's tragedy was that his " dearest mistress " should gradually outgrow the predominant influence that he had exercised over her mind during the heyday of their friendship. Yet, until it was an accomplished fact, he seems hardly to have noticed the change that was occurring. He did not understand that Mrs. Thrale's temperament had needs he himself could not hope to satisfy. He could not predict that the middle-aged woman who in *Thraliana* repeatedly boasts that she has never been in love —" As My Peace has never been disturbed by the *soft Passion* (she was writing optimistically in 1777), so it seldom comes in my head to talk of it "—would fall victim to a sudden romantic brain storm, that her love for the dark-eyed, sweet-tempered Italian singer, Gabriel Mario Piozzi, would obsess her to the exclusion of every other sentiment.

At this distance, the tremendous rumpus over Mrs. Thrale's second marriage seems remarkably unreasonable; and it is equally hard to sympathise with the prudish

stupefaction of Fanny Burney, the fury of the self-righteous
and disapproving daughters or the high-minded indignation
expressed by Mrs. Chapone and other learned but fashionable females, who considered that, by affording the public
the spectacle of an intelligent and well-bred woman hopelessly in love, she had done serious damage to the credit of
" the Bas Bleu Ladies." Mrs. Thrale's own feelings in the
matter, and the period of agonised perplexity through which
she passed, are amply displayed among the pages of
Thraliana. " Adieu to all that's dear, to all that's lovely
(wails the distracted woman, on the 29th of January, 1783).
I am parted from my Life, my Soul! my Piozzi: Sposo
promesso, Amante adorato! Amica senza equale." There
was a dreadful moment too, when Mrs. Thrale (who could
write cheerfully in 1778 that " as I never was a fond Wife,
so I certainly never was a Jealous one ") believed—quite
without cause—that Piozzi was paying attention to an
unmarried girl. But later volumes once again make it
completely clear that, although the world could not forgive
Mrs. Thrale for her marriage to a singer and foreigner, she
herself never regretted the decision she had taken, and that
her devotion to Piozzi ended only with his life. She had been
first attracted to him, during Thrale's lifetime, because he
reminded her of her father; and with him she seems to have
achieved a completeness of felicity hitherto undreamed of.

Her book, moreover, has that sharp, pleasing, individual
tang so characteristic of the literature of the English
eighteenth century. Here, beside the portrait of the artist
(conveyed unconsciously in a hundred small touches, and
also drawn by her own hand in a full-length " character ")
are innumerable thumbnail sketches of friends and enemies.
She gives us Goldsmith to the life, at his most fatuous and
inquisitive:

Doctor Goldsmith was certain a Man extremely odd: the first Time he dined with us, he gravely asked Mr. Thrale how much a Year he got by his Business? Who answered with singular Propriety, we don't talk of those things much in Company Doctor—but I hope to have the honour of knowing you so well that I shall wonder less at the Question.

and elsewhere:

The Doctor's Curiosity was as drole as his Vanity: he saw a great Cedar Chest in my House once—& nothing would serve him but to know what was within: I was from home it seems—his Visit was to Johnson. What makes you so uneasy says Mr. Johnson—why says he I long to pick the Lock of that Chest so—do dear Mr. Johnson look if none of your Keys will undo it.

Or she is told, and immediately jots down, an anecdote illustrative of the Reverend Laurence Sterne's views on marriage:

Says a Gentleman who listen'd while Sterne was abusing Matrimony—Come, Come, Jesus Christ once honoured a Wedding with his presence—but between You & I Sir replies Sterne, that was not the *best* thing he ever did.

Now she writes of wits and now of misers; now she fills a page or two with assorted medical lore—the case of Dr. Wall's daughter, a " fine straight healthy Girl " till she " accidentally swallowed a Brass Button which produced a Train of dreadful Symptoms in Succession for 8 years," and the prowess of " Evans the famous Man for curing Worms at Knightsbridge "; now she remarks on the colour and expression of different people's eyes:

My Eyes after all are not expressive ones. . . . The most piercing Eyes I ever saw were my Mother's, Garrick's, and Wedderburn the Counsellor's. . . . For sweetness mingled with Vivacity no Eyes ever equalled the famous Lady Coventry's. . . . The Eyes of the famous Courtezan Kitty Fischer, being of a Species quite apart, deserve to be mention'd: their Colour was of a Sky Blue, like a Ribbon, I never saw so beautiful a Brilliant Blue. . . .

So from 1776 to 1809, through periods of intense happiness, profound depression, hope, anxiety, despair, Mrs. Thrale's pen dashes busily and boldly forward. She was not to put it down till death had parted her from her adored second husband, as she records in two last pathetic entries:

Feb. 1809. No Birthday kept, no Pleasure, no Comfort: poor Piozzi seems merely kept alive by Opium & Brandy. . . . Something dreadful will I fear ensue.— *Must* Ensue:

30 *March* 1809. Everything most dreadful *has* ensued, —all is over; & my second Husband's Death is the last Thing recorded in my first husband's Present!

Yet, on the whole, life had been kind to her; and for herself she did not fear death. Its approaches were gradual. " I am happy to say she *knew* us (wrote Queeney during her mother's closing days) and appeared pleased at our being by Her Bed Side, & whenever she is awake she puts out a Hand to each of us. . . ." The cold censorious daughters had been at length forgiven; but the irrepressible vivacity and endearing " bad taste " were not quite extinguished. When her old favourite, Dr. Gibbes, paid her a concluding visit, she perpetrated the last pleasantry she would ever achieve. ". . . She had just strength to trace with her fingers the outline of a coffin in the air."

John Cam Hobhouse

In whose biography are you and I destined to provide an incidental footnote? Among our variously gifted friends, which man of talent, as we consider him now, will be saluted by future critics as recognisably a man of genius, with the result that public curiosity swoops on his associates and, after a long period of grateful obscurity, we are hounded back into the daylight? To see Shelley plain was a dangerous privilege: you might be vaguely haloed as a " Magnetic Lady," but you might also share the fate of poor tawdry Harriet and diabolical Miss Hitchener. Byron, too, made many posthumous victims; but, while the strange illumination that he shed picked out in cruel relief the folly and absurdity of most of the women he loved or who decided that they loved him, to the men he knew it has been less unkind; for, whereas he was inclined to choose his mistresses at random, or to allow himself to be chosen by any moderately attractive she-rake determined enough to wear down his resistance, in masculine friendships he used both heart and head, and was not ashamed to give free play to his more generous impulses. Thus a biographer, before he has done, grows desperately sick of Lady Caroline and Countess Guiccioli (who seem, now and then, not so much individuals as crude personifications of the Feminine Principle at its silliest and deadliest), but remains tolerant of Leigh Hunt and warmly attached to Matthews and Moore, Douglas

JOHN CAM HOBHOUSE
by Richard Dighton, 1819

Kinnaird and Scrope Davies. As for Hobhouse, though it is difficult not to laugh at him and at rare moments almost loathe him, there was something about that shy, pompous, egotistical, tactless but upright and well-meaning personage which, after a time, must recommend him to a modern reader's sympathy.

We feel wiser and gayer for having made his acquaintance; and, had he no connection with the life of Byron, John Cam Hobhouse, elevated to the peerage as Lord Broughton in 1851, would to-day lie at peace within the pages of the *Dictionary of National Biography*, decently interred under several massive paragraphs. But during the opening decade of the nineteenth century, John Cam, eldest son of Sir Benjamin Hobhouse, a rich commercial baronet, went up as Pensioner to Trinity College, Cambridge, and there caught sight of a pale-faced, curly-headed young man whom he resented at the first glance. Lord Byron was wearing a white hat and a grey coat and riding a grey horse—an assemblage of colours that Hobhouse, always touchy in matters of convention, would appear to have stigmatised as affected and ungentlemanly; and he did not overcome his original prejudice till the summer of 1807, when he had examined a copy of Byron's early verses, and both young enthusiasts had joined the Cambridge Whig Club. From that stage, a friendship quickly developed, flourishing, as friendships are apt to do, on their extreme dissimilarity, and refreshed and enlivened by numerous tiffs and squabbles. Byron possessed an extraordinary fascination, did he care to exercise it: Hobhouse was relatively lacking in charm, but was not without wit and a certain trenchant shrewdness. Byron, the product of a long line of violent and unhappy prodigals, was a fatalist and an immoralist, haunted by a sense of guilt; and Hobhouse, beneath his worldly trappings, preserved many of the virtues of his solid merchant forebears. Yes, he was *solid*—that was the appropriate adjective. Broad-shouldered and brief in stature—Cobbett once called him " little Sancho," and Hobhouse by way of retaliation endeavoured to knock the reformer down—he had a wide forehead, an aquiline nose, a substantial and aggressive chin. Not that he was in the least a prig. Charles Skinner Matthews, the " Citoyen," whom Byron would afterwards describe as an intellectual giant, professed atheist, free-liver and master of the daring paradox, might fluster and disconcert, but could not wholly floor, him. With Scrope Davies he gambled and drank; and, when he accompanied his Cambridge boon-companions, with their assorted " house-holds and whore-holds," on a visit to the seaside, he plunged boldly into the raffish pleasures of Brighton, emerging none the worse for wear, if somewhat dizzy and exhausted, having consumed far too much champagne and hock, and, during the course of an intoxicated quarrel, attacked Davies with a table-knife. . . .

Yet in essence he remained profoundly respectable—a righteous, even on occasions a slightly censorious representative of the liberal-minded upper-middle class. Hence the peculiarity, and the constant vicissitudes, of his relationship with Byron, who, albeit less aristocratic than he liked to imagine and considerably less satanic than he sometimes chose to bruit about, was as reckless of his reputation as his fabulous grand-uncle, " The Wicked Lord." But, although it underwent a variety of changes, Hobhouse's attitude towards his fascinating friend was never sanctimonious or insensitive. He appreciated Byron's astonishing qualities, and was prepared to attribute to him a degree of moral worth that the poet's conduct of his private life did not often seem to justify: he refused, on the other hand, to settle down into the rôle of tame admirer. A naturally obstinate and self-centred man, far from appearing to welcome the attentions of a wayward child of genius, he could not himself always restrain a tone of half-impatient patronage. Byron might be a wonderfully good companion; but Childe Harold, or Byron in the Childe Harold mood, frequently offended against his native common sense. Worse still, the " dear fellow " occasionally behaved in a most un-English manner! At the jovial debauchery of Cambridge and Brighton and London, Hobhouse, sceptic and man of the world, showed no disposition to raise a disapproving eyebrow; but, once the two of them had set out for Turkey and Greece, where the travellers were cut off from wholesome English influences, he observed with dismay that his friend's habits became more and more bohemian, and that he tended to pick up remarkably dubious cronies and queer Levantine hangers-on. In fact, their joint tour was not entirely harmonious; yet they managed to get through it without an open quarrel; and, while Byron was only moderately reluctant to say good-bye to Hobhouse, John Cam experienced a pang of regret that obviously surprised him, and which in his wary, inhibited fashion he did his best to smile away. " Took leave (he noted drily in his private journal) *non sine lacrymis*, of this singular young person on a little stone terrace . . . at the end of the bay, dividing with him a little nosegay of flowers; perhaps the last thing that I shall ever divide with him." But the island of Zea was not the end of their pilgrimage; and in mid-July, 1811, Hobhouse learned that Byron was expected home. " Welcome," he wrote in Latin, "will be the arrival of the hour unhoped for," and in English: " Thank God you are not, as Fletcher . . . told me you were, gone to *Pallantine in Egypt*."

A year later, *Childe Harold* was published; and the singular young person, getting more singular and more moody as the days went on, opened his eyes to discover that he was now a famous poet. It must be remembered to Hobhouse's advantage that, although his own literary efforts had proved completely fruitless, he was able to withstand the vulgar pricks of envy. The line that he adopted was understanding and protective, rather than competitive. With Lady Caroline pleading and storming, and her mother, Lady Bessborough (whom Byron had nicknamed "Lady Blarney") loudly expostulating in the middle distance, while Melbourne House rocked to its foundations; and even the Prince Regent, as a former devotee of Lady Melbourne, felt constrained to put a word in, making " diabolick " suggestions about Byron's sexual temperament, before long the puzzled protector found he had his hands full. The levity of his friend's fashionable acquaintances was constantly embarrassing, sometimes downright shocking. Lady Bessborough had asked him to call: when " in the midst of our conversation in comes Lady C. Lamb, who talked of Lady Bessborough and myself looking guilty. Here's pass for the world to come to." Lady Oxford, who had supplanted Lady Caroline, was nearly as unnerving; for, though exceedingly civil to a shy young man, she was also " most uncommon in her talk, and licentious "; and her daughter, Lady Jane Harley, whom Hobhouse was inclined to adore, struck him as " a delightful creature " but, regrettably, " *un peu libre*." By Lady Caroline he was frankly appalled and disgusted; and his private journal[1] contains a diverting account of one of her many piratical descents on Byron's London lodgings, the small rooms that he inhabited above a hatter's shop in Bennet Street. The friends had planned to set out for Harrow; but at noon a succession of thunderous raps shook the panels of the front door. They saw a crowd in the street below, and " immediately a person in a most strange disguise walked up-

[1]Extracts from unpublished portions appeared for the first time in the latest biography of Hobhouse, *My Friend H*. By Michael Joyce. Murray.

stairs; it turned out to be the Lady in question from Brocket. She, seeing me, ran up the garret stairs on which I went down into Mr. Dollman's shop and ordered a hat. ...." A less staunch character might have taken to flight, reflecting as he escaped down St. James's Street that, after all, Lady Caroline's importunities were none of his concern. But Hobhouse gallantly returned to the fray, peremptorily forbade an elopement (which the unfortunate lover had promised as an alternative to suicide), soothed the indignant landlord downstairs, ordered Fletcher, Byron's valet, to keep a sharp watch on the bedroom, borrowed a housemaid's bonnet and shoes, performed miracles with hackney-coaches and finally deposited Lady Caroline upon a neutral doorstep. " God knows (he concluded) that from the very beginning I have done my best to keep my friend out of the scrape. My first wish was that he should give this lady ... no power over him by consenting to any serious folly, and when I knew everything had passed between them, my next desire was to prevent a public disclosure and an elopement. This latter event would, as B. assured me and assures me, have certainly taken place but for the part I played in the transactions of yesterday. ...."

Well, the dear misguided fellow had scrambled out of his scrape—a stroke of good luck for which John Cam, quite justifiably, was prepared to claim some credit. Byron was not impossible to manage if one loved and understood him; and for a while Hobhouse remained firmly convinced that the disturbing rumours which began to circulate were altogether baseless. Then in 1816 Lady Byron left home; and he found himself head over heels in a far deeper, darker scandal. At first he resolutely declined to believe that the " Princess of Parallelograms " had any genuine grievance—his old friend delighted in mystification, and was apt to indulge a somewhat distorted sense of humour; but when the poet's half-sister and his cousin, who had been the unwilling spectators of distressful scenes at Piccadilly Terrace, described "very great tyranny, menaces, furies, neglects and even real injuries," he felt obliged to accuse Byron of some degree of double-dealing and "got him to own much of what I had been told. . . . He was dreadfully agitated, said he was ruined and would blow out his brains. He, indignant but yet terrified sometimes, says ' and yet she loved me once,' and at other times that he is glad to be quit of such a woman. . . . I took leave of my poor friend—Alas! what a ruin."

Although his faith in Byron had been severely shaken, their friendship persisted without further serious mishaps till the spring of 1824, when early one May morning he received the news from Missolonghi. Byron's death caused him " an agony of grief such as I have experienced only twice before in my life—once when I lost my dear friend, Charles Skinner Matthews, and afterwards when at Paris I heard that my brother Benjamin had been killed at Quatre Bras. . . ." In July, the body returned to England; and Hobhouse, who had originally refused to approach it, at length followed Kinnaird towards the open coffin. Slowly approaching, he had a glimpse of the features. " Distorted, discoloured, and grotesque, they retained not a trace of the living Byron. . . ." Having bidden this ghastly farewell, and closed the most stimulating chapter of a long and active life-story, he swung back to the world of practical affairs, from which the spectacle of Byron's rise and fall had intermittently distracted him. He lived to be eighty-three, married comfortably, begat children, inherited his father's large fortune and held high public office. The fervent radicalism of his youth was gradually replaced by a very moderate type of liberalism, and some of his early allies were apt to murmur that Hobhouse was a renegade; yet the lineaments of the juvenile Hobhouse never completely disappeared. Pompous and humourless he may often have been; but beneath the obstinacy and self-assertion lurked a touching sensitiveness, complicated by a strain of almost morbid diffidence. Naturally warm-hearted, he was always afraid of emotion; and his usual tendency was to minimise the value and importance of his own feelings. In consequence, he frequently strikes us as churlish and ungracious; and, when after much gloomy debate he finally decided to venture into marriage, his treatment of his bethrothed showed Hobhouse at his least romantic, so determined was he not to exaggerate the quality of his affection for her. That his was a *mariage de raison* he firmly insisted. Lady Julia Hay was not very young, nor (one deduces) disturbingly attractive; but she came of a rich and distinguished family, and seemed (Hobhouse remarked) " a most amiable, well-disposed person," whose combination of breeding and virtue could scarcely fail to do him credit. During the first weeks of their marriage, his journal received a characteristic entry: " In public matters . . . I do think I am as honest as a man can be in an unreformed Parliament. It has come round to me from several quarters that Julia says she enjoys perfect happiness; some folk are easily pleased." Yet the concluding sneer was aimed rather at himself than at the devoted Lady Julia, whom at her death he was to describe as the pride and treasure of his heart, and whom during her lifetime he loved and cherished faithfully. For in the depths of his mind hid a demon of doubt; and that doubting demon was perhaps another form of good angel. Many charges may be brought against Hobhouse: some telling criticisms have been made by his biographer: but one uncommon and endearing trait appears in the record of all his words and actions. He was solemn and sententious: yet he was rarely smug. A rich, respectable and respected man, to the end of his existence he did not acquire complacency.

George Bryan Brummell

ONE WINTRY morning, early in 1838, there arrived at the Hotel d'Angleterre in Caen an English lady, soberly dressed but of patrician manners, who requested an interview with the landlord upon private business. She understood (she said) that a compatriot of hers was M. Fichet's inmate. She was anxious to catch a glimpse of him, but—here came the difficulty—she must see him while she herself remained invisible! Nothing could be simpler, replied the landlord. At five o'clock precisely every evening M. Brummell descended to the *table d'hôte* from the apartments that he occupied on the third floor. If the lady cared to engage a room, M. Fichet promised to detain him outside her door for a few minutes' conversation. Punctuality, it appeared, was M. Brummell's *forte*; and that evening, exactly at the moment named, dragging footsteps sounded on the upper staircase, answered from below by those of the landlord. Carrying a candlestick and wrapped in a cloak, a decrepit figure shuffled slowly into view, quavering but ceremonious and dimly dignified. His salutation of the landlord was polite and impassive. Though his clothes were in the last stage of threadbare misery, and from a venerable wig oil dripped down on to his coat-collar, though his cheeks were toothless and sunken and his mouth distorted, around him hung that indefinable air of greatness which belongs to the natural leader, the born creator.

When M. Fichet returned to his other English guest, he found her weeping so bitterly and unrestrainedly that it was some time before she could collect her faculties and pay the bill. Then she departed at once for Paris, leaving no name behind. Her identity has never been established; and one can only imagine that an early adorer—a victim of that ambiguous, almost poetic charm which the great Beau often exercised upon the opposite sex—was seeking to lay the ghost of her remembered passion. If that was her object, she must have succeeded far too thoroughly. Or it may be that, by the light of a brutal contrast, the portrait retained by her memory seemed fresher and clearer—more seductive in its faintly smiling, good-natured insolence. It was a portrait, essentially, of a previous age; and meanwhile manners had changed and life rushed forward. Few men have been more completely superannuated; and by March 30, 1840, when a watching nun at the public asylum of Le Bon Sauveur noticed upon the old man's exhausted face an expression of " intense fear and anxiety " and the long decline sharpened to an abrupt conclusion, friends, lovers, admirers had all deserted him. Some were dead, some ruined and some forgetful. The very society he had ornamented had passed away: a world tamer and more decorous was now in the making.

Baudelaire's essay, " *Le Peintre de la Vie Moderne*," besides his personal philosophy of dandyism, includes some special references to dandyism and English life. Such extravagances have a deep root in our national temperament: they are the product (at least according to the romantic view) of the mingled cynicism and sentiment of the Anglo-Saxon nature, with its intransigent individualism and fundamental, ineradicable eccentricity. No other race has the bravado to be so entirely odd! And the true Dandy needs the kind of courage, tinged with impertinence and backed up by a cool contempt for his fellow-men, that is only bred among the fogs and damps of *Ultima Thule*. Where else could Beau Brummell have worked out his fate? In what other country could a man, whose grandfather had been a valet and had afterwards made a livelihood by letting lodgings, have achieved an altitude from which he dominated patrician society and gave lessons in deportment to the Prince of Wales? Nor had Brummell risen by any obvious effort. Like many Englishmen he preferred to succeed as it were in spite of himself—casually, unselfconsciously, in the manner born. London awoke and found Brummell famous. Brummell accepted its recognition with smiling *savoir vivre*.

The Dandy is never shocked and never delighted. Indeed, it is his immunity from commonplace passions that makes it possible for him to impose himself upon society and carry egotism to a point where it is almost disinterested. He is intensely self-centred, yet also a stoic: for what moves him (as Baudelaire suggests in his essay) is not a vulgar concern with self-adornment, which measures its satisfaction by the approval of others, but a worship of perfection that is its own reward. Dandies, Baudelaire declared, usually rose during periods of transition—Brummell, for instance, a man of plebeian birth who sprang to the surface during a period of war and change, and became a brilliant parodist of aristocratic foibles. He was an imitator but, through force of genius, a consummate innovator. He had discovered (as many dandies before and since: Beau Nash was a fine example) that the pride which often accompanies exalted birth is curiously susceptible to the charms of insolence, and that one of the greatest pleasures of the brainless but haughty lies in being humbled. Hence the conversational methods

72

he always adopted—his style (to quote the words of a
modern essayist) " flickering, sneering, hovering on the
verge of insolence, skimming the edge of nonsense, but
always keeping within some curious mean." *Nothing too
much* was the dictum he followed. Too much wit is anti-
social because it is overpowering; and Brummell specialised
in the type of half-way pleasantry that is the more amusing
because it is accompanied by a flavour of pointlessness. His
sallies were deliberately unemphatic. Asked on his return
from a country house what kind of people he had been
visiting, " Don't ask me," Brummell sighed. " In my bedroom I actually found a cobweb in my pot! " When another
friend sympathised during an attack of gout, " The worst
of it is," said Brummell, " it is my favourite leg! " and
when he caught a bad cold between London and Brighton,
" The landlord " (explained Brummell to a solicitous
intimate) " put me in a room with a damp stranger."

Similarly, his *brusquerie* was tinged with kindness, and
his approbation, now and then, had the bite of a sneer.
Above all things, he was individual and unexpected—cool,
clear-headed, undogmatic. Nature itself in forming the
person of George Bryan Brummell seemed to have obeyed
the same spirit of moderation, for he was neither (like
Hervey) improbably handsome nor (like Chesterfield) uncommonly hard featured. His face was long and expressive
and extremely mobile, the eyes grey, the nose aquiline
(though squashed and broken), the hair fine and abundant,
the forehead lofty. A drawing by Robert Dighton, executed
at the period of his greatest success, shows us Brummell as
he may have appeared at the age of twenty-seven. One hand
grasps hat and stick with an easy gesture: the other hand,
placed negligently upon the hip, plays with the fingers of a
single glove. Tight breeches are completed by tasselled
hessians; while a tail coat, which emphasises the shoulders

73

and hints at the waist, is crowned by the protuberance of a perfect neckcloth, swelling up to the extremity of the dandy's chin. We do not forget that the boots had blackened soles and that the neckcloth's tie was only achieved after hours of labour. We remember that he left his dressing-room in a cushioned sedan chair and was deposited—a previous *bibelot*—at the foot of the staircase or on the very threshold of the gathering which he was concerned to dazzle.

About such a wardrobe there is nothing ludicrous. In fact, it was Brummell's realism in the matter of clothes that made him so magnificent an exponent of the art of dressing. Brummell's inclination ran to blacks and whites, to buffs and blues and broadcloths and spotless linen, all arranged in an immaculate Whistlerian symphony. The perceptive eye leaped at propriety and was proud to recognise it. The Dandy's costume was superbly suitable and little more. Ostentation by such standards is the height of vulgarity. Yet, though Brummell's mind was certainly not vulgar, there are the seeds of its decline in every triumph. However complete his domination over her royal lover, Brummell should not have attempted to snub Mrs. Fitzherbert, or at least not made a joke that enshrined his antagonism. For the Prince Regent was soon flustered, easily wounded; and, while he might have forgiven Beau Brummell's reference to himself as " Big Ben," " Benina " was an unforgivable insult, a direct challenge to the *amour propre* of a royal personage. George's revenge was deliberate and long premeditated. Magnanimity had never been one of his attributes: and he took no steps to arrest the progress of his companion's ruin and was at no pains to alleviate Beau Brummell's misery. That he failed to forget Brummell was an undoubted compliment; but when he remembered him it was in no spirit of indulgence or charity.

The Beau's fall occurred on May 17, 1816 (the same

year that saw the social collapse of Byron), and from the consequences of that fall he failed to rally. Contributory were Beau Brummell's gambling habits. Again and again his friends dissuaded him; but, although Brummell had won £26,000 during the year 1813 and nearly doubled his always meagre capital, he refused their suggestions that he should buy an annuity. So fortunate and accomplished a man need not expect to lose. Besides, he loved the " rattle and dash of the dice-box," the late hours, the masochistic thrill of losing, the sheer fun of dismissing his losses with a smile and a pleasantry. He did not count with the new gamblers of 1816, crude and hardened veterans of Napoleon's wars, who brought a military keenness into the pursuit of punting. Brummell lost heavily and lost repeatedly. He tried in vain to recoup himself by devious stratagems— Lord Worcester supplied him with £7,000; Meyler, the moneylender, was exceedingly serviceable. Yet the end came; and there was nothing that he could do but fly the country.

Exile, for some years, was not unpleasant. Thirty-eight —but confident that, were it not for the ravages of " care and distress " upon his " unfortunate phiz," he would have no difficulty in passing for " *five-and-twenty* "—he continued to keep up with the London world. His old friends visited him from time to time; and Harriette Wilson in 1823, a faded courtesan living on the proceeds of blackmail, discovered him, when she called, wearing a Florentine dressing-gown and attended by " just such a valet as one would have given the Beau in the acme of his glory, well powdered, very ceremonious." Brummell, who looked plump and fresh and cheerful, begged to be allowed to go on shaving—which he did " with a peculiar grace " and the smallest razor Harriette had ever seen, talking as he worked away of his dog and his furniture and the " green silk shoe " that had been presented him by a Parisian actress. Altogether, he seemed self-confident and entirely unashamed. " From what I had heard," said the spiteful Harriette, " I fully expected to have found him reclined on a couch, worn down to a skeleton." The Beau was courteous, evasive, charming; and here we come to a significant aspect of Beau Brummell's character. There is no evidence for the imputation that he was homosexual: there is every reason, in spite of many desultory love-affairs, to imagine that he was profoundly narcissistic—in other words, almost incapable of normal passion. More than any man or woman, he adored himself. No mistress can be discovered for him, among high or low. Women often loved him and men admired him: but he was curiously diffident in making contacts and always prompt with an excuse if entanglement threatened, though prolific of fine sentiments when there was no such danger. At least twice it seemed probable that he might become engaged; and with remarkable circumspection he managed to slip free, covering up his retreat with a diverting witticism. For example, Lady Mary had encroached on his liberty: and, though nobly born, she was not a person he desired to marry. " What could I do but cut the connection? " he observed to an intimate. " I discovered that Lady Mary actually ate cabbage! "

The cabbage-eaters grew more numerous as time proceeded; and Brummell little by little became more tolerant. His penniless life at Calais was a kind of slumber. The vivid, lively, ironic, laughing Dandy sank first of all into a vegetable kindliness—" I am still vegetating (he wrote in 1829) . . . with the fat weeds that sleep within the stagnant ditches that surround this place. I am indeed comparatively as fat . . ."—then sauntered down the long decline towards senility. After Calais, he obtained a Consular post at Caen and embarked on a course of retrenchments that were destructive of luxury; but a washerwoman still took a third of his tiny income and three shirts a day was his normal allowance, besides gallons of hair oil and quarts of blacking. But what he could not buy he had started to borrow; and when he could not borrow with dignity he had begun to cadge.

A last glimpse of the authentic Beau at his toilette reaches us through Captain Jesse, who visited him at Caen in February 1832. Having washed himself in milk-and-water for a couple of hours, Brummell applied himself to the extraction of superfluous hairs with a minute dentist's mirror. The clothes that he assumed were as quiet in hue as always—a " snuff-coloured surtout, with a velvet collar . . . a real cashmere waistcoat, made from a shawl which . . . must have cost a hundred guineas . . . dark-blue trousers, very pointed boots, the unrivalled white neckcloth, a black hat larger at the crown than the circumference of his head, and primrose kid gloves." Under his arm he carried a brown silk umbrella, " the handle . . . surmounted by the head of George the Fourth in ivory, with well-curled wig and smiling graciously." His only jewellery was a ring dug up on the Field of the Cloth of Gold and " a massive chain of Venetian ducat gold," of which he exhibited never more than two links. In the street, fearing to disturb his coiffure, he made a point of not taking off his hat, even to a lady; " in fine weather, the salute of his associates was acknowledged by a bow, or, if on the other side of the street, by an extension of his arm, and a slight movement of his fingers in the air "; and, thus covered, he would tiptoe with a slight stoop over the muddy cobbles of the Rue St. Jean, bidding his companion, who walked behind him, be sure to keep his distance, that no speck of mud might spoil the harmony of the bankrupt Beau's *ensemble*. . . .

Alas, he would not remain a Beau much longer. Not

many years separated him from complete senility, from the degradation and squalor of a premature breakdown. The story of his last years makes tragic reading. It might serve as a *memento mori* to any æsthete in whom the love of beauty is more enduring than the fear of death, and in whom the pride of intelligence seems to defy extinction. Yet, at the same time, they are a justification of the Dandy's effort. " Only those who already know the value of the useless can be talked to about the useful," said a Taoist sage of the third century before Christ. Only those who have themselves suffered in the cause of perfection can appreciate the destiny of Beau Brummell—" poor Brummell," the oddest and greatest and saddest of the Dandies.

Charles Greville

BORN IN the mid-decades of the eighteenth century, with similar talents, to the same position and opportunity, Charles Greville might have been a happier and a duller man. But fate fixed his birth in 1794; romantic elements found their way into his composition; and, though to outward appearances the perfect *homme du monde*, successful at Newmarket and lucky in love, beneath the surface he was far from ordinary and by no means self-satisfied. The façade he presented was an entirely deceptive one. At a very early age, his maternal grandfather, the Duke of Portland, had secured for him both the Secretaryship " in reversion " of the Island of Jamaica and a Clerkship Extraordinary to the Privy Council; with the result that an easily earned and sufficient income was supplied him, at the public expense, to the end of his days. He enjoyed racing, company, travel; and he could certainly afford them. His face itself, with its hooked nose, small critical eye and sardonic lower lip—the mask of a Regency frequenter of White's and the Jockey Club—conceals the complexity of that difficult and curious temperament. He had most advantages that apparently make for happiness: many different triumphs might have ministered to his self-esteem—he rejected them and remained obstinately convinced of failure.

It is to this conviction that we owe his famous Memoirs.

Beginning them again on January 2, 1838, Greville observes, in a mood of characteristic self-denigration, that " it seems exceedingly ridiculous to say that one strong stimulus proceeds from reading Scott's Diary—which he began very late in life and in consequence of reading Byron's—not because I fancy that I can write a diary as amusing as Scott's or Byron's, but because I am struck by the excessive pleasure which Scott appeared to derive from writing his journal, and I am (and this is the principal cause) struck with the important use to which the habit may be turned. The habit of recording is first of all likely to generate a desire to have something of some interest to record . . . it will exercise the memory and sharpen the understanding generally; and though the thoughts may not be very profound, nor the remarks very lively and ingenious, or the narrative of exceeding interest, still the exercise is, I think, calculated to make the writer wiser and perhaps better."

His journal, though at the time he could not bring himself to believe that it possessed any permanent value, was, in fact, a means of justifying his continued existence in his own eyes and of raising a bulwark against the bitter remorse that perpetually assailed him. His closest friends can scarcely have suspected the inward struggle; and, when they learned that he had won four thousand pounds at Newmarket, they must have congratulated him as a bold and clever plunger, little imagining that, as soon as he returned home, he would open one of the red morocco volumes to which he committed the record of his day-to-day life and burst out in a strain of passionate self-condemnation:

" For many weeks past (he writes during the June of 1835) I have been out of the way of society and politics. . . . When for a time all other books are abandoned for the betting book, when I herd with the vilest and stupidest and most degraded of beings, and am occupied with the mysteries and craft of the stable to the exclusion of all other interests, pursuits and occupants, I am also tormented with a sensation of self-reproach, of shame and of remorse, which is exactly akin to what the drunkard feels in his sober intervals. . . . If this is the case why don't I give it up anybody might ask. Because in spite of these feelings I like the amusement, the excitement . . . I have no sufficient temptation in any other quarter. I cannot find throughout the range of existence any other object probably *attainable* commensurate with the sacrifice."

Greville's self-reproaches have a vehemence, a frequency, a repetitious intensity, seldom surpassed except perhaps by those of Coleridge. He was devoted to the idea of self-improvement. No doubt he was a favoured guest at Holland House. No doubt, both there and elsewhere, he had conversed upon terms of complete equality with some of the most brilliant and most gifted men of the time. He was indifferent to his social successes as to his racing victories: nothing could persuade him that he was not weak and wicked and dissipated. A regular diary was his only hope, his sole salvation; and so a new pen was sharpened and the candles were lit.

It was not till November 13, 1860, as an old, infirm, crusty and eccentric bachelor, that Charles Greville, after an interval of three months, finally took his pen in hand " to record my determination to bring this journal (which is no journal at all) to an end," closing it, he added, " with a full consciousness of the smallness of its value or interest, and with great regret that I did not make better use of the opportunities I have had. . . ." In spite of these gloomy forebodings, however, he decided to bequeath his ninety-one slim quarto note-books to an old friend and colleague, Henry Reeve, and allow his executor to publish parts of them as he thought fit. Reeve's first two volumes, covering the reigns of George IV and William IV appeared, nine years after Greville's death, in 1874; and the Queen, who had previously sent a message of personal condolence to his brother Henry, speaking of the dead man " with peculiar kindness," declared that she was "*horrified* and *indignant*. . . ." The diarist's " indiscretion, indelicacy, ingratitude towards friends, betrayal of confidence and shameful disloyalty towards the Sovereign make it *very important* that the book should be severely censured and discredited "; to which her Prime Minister (who had himself no cause to love Greville) replied that " Your Majesty's critique on the Greville publications ought to be printed. It condenses the whole case. . . . The book is a social outrage . . ."

Though " The Greville Memoirs " have long ceased to be considered a social outrage, a certain atmosphere of mystery continued to cling to them. What of the passages omitted? Were they " printable "? If the work were ever published in complete form, might it not still be necessary to retain the diarist's original modest cipher? When, at last, we could reply to these questions, and had the whole of Greville laid before us, in eight volumes,[1] without suppression or emendation, apart from perhaps a very few, relatively unimportant sentences it proved to contain little that could not be read aloud to a bench of bishops. Greville was more nice and scrupulous than we had ever supposed. He was stern—almost too stern—in his attitude towards personal gossip and social scandal. He laboured to include nothing that did not possess real and solid interest. He had, moreover, high ideals of the diarist's function. A " journal to be good, true, and interesting (he decides at the beginning

[1] *The Greville Memoirs, 1814-1860.* Edited by Lytton Strachey and Roger Fulford. Macmillan.

of 1838) should be written without the slightest reference to publication, but without any fear of it; it should be the transcript of a mind which can bear transcribing." That pronouncement is Greville's own best eulogium. His Memoirs are, indeed, the transcript of a mind that need have no fear of transcription—not a mind very original or very profound, gifted with any particular spiritual *finesse*, but admirably well equipped for the purposes of a shrewd observer.

The effect of the complete Greville is impressively spacious. Greville has the faculty, peculiar to good diarists, of providing a panoramic view of past events, so that we live through them with some of the excitement of actual experience, yet are able to judge of them in terms of their historic upshot. Here, it must be admitted, Greville was lucky—fortunate, that is to say, as a diarist, though his position was often uncomfortable as a human being. Born in the reign of George III, he lived to see the Regency, the accession of George IV, the bustling incursion of William IV, the arrival of Victoria and the growing ascendancy of the Prince Consort. As a representative of the old order, he was sometimes short-sighted; as a judge of character, he was in most instances extremely shrewd; and his obituary portraits are among his most brilliant achievements. William IV, Madame de Lieven, Lady Holland, Lord Melbourne, Lord Hertford, the Duke of Wellington—each is described with a sharpness and neatness, yet with an economy of words and a sobriety of phrasing, that a professional historian might be inclined to envy. And where, as in his dealings with Queen Victoria, he had not the chance of finally summarising his observations, his scattered notes have a cumulative vividness that is no less remarkable.

An anthology might be put together of Greville's references to one of the most puzzling, interesting and exasperating of English sovereigns. The Duke of Clarence had been a refreshing change after his elder brother:

"What a *changement de décoration* (writes the diarist in June, 1831); no longer George the 4th, capricious, luxurious, and misanthropic, liking nothing but the society of listeners and flatterers, with the Conyngham tribe and one or two Tory Ministers and Foreign Ambassadors; but a plain, vulgar, hospitable gentleman, opening his doors to all the world, with a numerous family and suite . . . a Whig Minister, and no foreigners, and no toad-eaters at all. Nothing more different, and looking at him one sees how soon this act will be finished, and the scene be changed for another probably not less dissimilar."

But the full oddity of the next change he could scarcely foresee, or that " our little Princess," glimpsed as " a short, vulgar-looking child " at a children's ball given by her uncle in 1829 and, afterwards, as a shadowy figure at her mother's side, would reappear, clad in virginal modesty but royal dignity, to astonish the world by her calm acceptance of an exalted position. Nor could he have prophesied the immediate sequel. On June 25, he remarks that " the Crown has been transferred to the head of the new Queen with a tranquillity that is curious and edifying ": but, five days later, having reported how the Queen has snubbed Madame de Lieven, annihilated the troublesome Sir John Conroy, and put her mother firmly but respectfully into her place, he adds that " in the midst of all her propriety of manner and conduct, the young Queen begins to exhibit slight signs of a peremptory disposition, and it is impossible not to suspect that as She gains confidence, and as her character begins to develope, She will evince a strong will of her own." Those " slight signs " soon grew more and more evident. In the disastrous affair of Lady Flora Hastings, and in the squabble with Peel over the Ladies of

the Bedchamber, she showed that she could be both obstinate
and wrong-headed, and a time came when her popularity
had sunk to zero. High hopes were succeeded for a while
by dark misgivings.

Existing as he had always done in the atmosphere of
power and privilege, it was not to be expected that Charles
Greville should have very much sympathy with, or indeed
make much attempt to understand, the various liberal
movements that agitated Europe. Thus, he was horrified by
the revolutions of 1848, and, while he deplored the condition
of the industrial populace—the grimy world of sweat-shops
and mines and furnaces, " the hot factory rooms " where
the women looked " very wan, very dirty, and one should
guess very miserable"—he had no patience with the ideology
of radical reformers. In such questions as these he remained
true to his upbringing. Yet, although it is easy to condemn
the social order that Greville represented, and though
Greville sometimes condemned that order himself, it is
difficult not to find many of its attributes praiseworthy.
To-day, when literary and political or social eminence
seldom go hand in hand, Greville's account of debates at
Holland House makes remarkable reading; and, after
attending a dinner party at Holland House, his self-
reproaches were apt to become particularly vehement and
he would reflect upon " the defects and omissions of my
early education " or concede bitterly that, " if the eyes
travel over the pages of a book, while the mind is far away
upon Newmarket Heath . . . the result can only be useless
imperfect information, crude and superficial ideas, constant
shame, and frequent disappointment and mortification."
But, by modern standards, Greville was a voracious reader
and to the end of his life remained intensely interested in the
things of the mind. He devoured every book, ancient or
modern, he could lay his hands on; and, at the close of the

year 1818, he announces that he has " read in the last few months—5 vols. of Gibbon—St. Simon—Marmontel's memoirs—Rousseau's confessions—Memoirs of Q. Eliz. —Lives of the Poets—Boswell's Life of Johnson "—" a solid achievement " (as his editor remarks) " for a fashionable young man of twenty-four."

Matthew Arnold

OF ALL the variously horrid forms in which sentence of annihilation has been passed on famous writers, none seems more unjust than that reserved for Matthew Arnold, who, during the spring of 1888, fell dead in a Liverpool street while running for a tramcar. The background, the occasion, the haste, the lack of dignity—all might have been contrived to make an inappropriate ending. It was as if the spirit of the 19th century, symbolised by a noisy mechanical juggernaut grinding towards the docks between shabby prosperous warehouses, had finally vanquished the gallant exponent of a less inharmonious order. But, though Arnold's life was a long and eloquent protest against contemporary social standards, the protest was delivered in his own way, with a moderation and even a kind of forbearance that set it apart from the comminations of other 19th-century critics. It bore no resemblance to Carlyle's hoarse cantankerous outcry —feelingly described in Arnold's most ambitious elegiac poem; and it showed no trace of the passionate exasperation, the tone of personal embitterment, that spoils much of Ruskin's later writing. Arnold retained his composure; and accounts of his conversation and physical appearance suggest a man with a gift for enjoyment and a belief in human happiness, who during his lifetime carried heavy burdens but did not always bear them gloomily. The late Logan

Pearsall-Smith, for example, once described how, on a tour of Germany, he had caught sight of the celebrated writer at a modest hotel dinner table. The young American was surprised and shocked; for he had expected, we understand, an air of solemn reverie, and Matthew Arnold's attitude was gay and almost flippant. Could *this* be the author of *Culture and Anarchy*? The gospel of sweetness and light had apparently been translated into a whiff of fragrant hair-oil. His waistcoat was far too conspicuous, his gloves somewhat too yellow, his abundant whiskers too ambrosial; he was conversing—and talking, Pearsall-Smith suspected, perhaps a little too audibly—about a visit he had just paid to certain aged local princesses. The sceptical and dandified undergraduate, Lord Lansdowne's bright young secretary, had not completely vanished in the grave Inspector of Schools or been entirely obliterated by years of incessant toil and impecunious marriage. His prophetic voice might be the voice of Empedocles: in his personality there was still a lingering touch of Callicles

Touching thy harp as the whim came on thee,
And prais'd and spoil'd by master and by guests.

—which a generation of comfortless railway journeys, chilly gas-light classrooms and laborious official reports could never quite extinguish.

Does this elasticity betray a lack of profundity? Such, at least, has been the impression formed by some of Arnold's readers. " Of Matthew Arnold as a philosopher (wrote Herbert W. Paul in the ' English Men of Letters ' series) it may be said that, though clear he was not deep, and that though gentle, he was not dull." The same criticism might be applied to his verse. Its beauty does not consist in the display of extreme originality: it contains no sudden tremendous glimpses into the life of man and nature: it has little of Tennysonian sweetness or stern Miltonic majesty. But at its finest it possesses a peculiar distinction; and, if we re-read Arnold without astonishment, the process usually includes some grateful re-discoveries. Given a properly receptive mood, we soon establish with the writer a close and sympathetic contact, echoing his plaints and subscribing to his aspirations:

> *A fugitive and gracious light he seeks,*
> *Shy to illumine; and I seek it too.*

As the poet flits ahead like his own Scholar Gipsy, the reader follows where he chooses to lead, not, it is true, on a surge of wild enthusiasm, but inspired by a sedate confidence that the pursuit will be rewarding. The objective may be a trifle hazy, the line of flight eccentric; but there is much to admire in the cultivated undulations of the rich surrounding landscape.

Re-reading implies re-valuation; and a new selection of Arnold's poems[1], prompts a tentative review of their essential poetic worth. The editor does not make extravagant claims for Matthew Arnold's genius; but " among English reflective poets " Mr. Dyment asserts that he deserves to take a high place, adding that " what Bede wrote of the monk Caedmon is also apt for him: ' . . . He whatsoever he could hear and learn would afterwards think upon the same again by himself, and chewing thereon like a clean beast at his cud, would turn it into very sweet metre.' " To have been compared to a Saxon monk or to a placid beast of the field might well have puzzled Arnold; yet Bede's phrase is unexpectedly neat, and helps, moreover, to distinguish this reflective poet from another poet of reflection to whom he has been elsewhere, not unfairly, likened. Gray and

[1] *Matthew Arnold.* An Introduction and a Selection. By Clifford Dyment. Phoenix House.

Arnold were both of a meditative turn, both at variance
with the world around them, but both restrained in the
protests they uttered as they were disciplined in the lives
they led. Neither of them was a bohemian, neither was a
revolutionary: Arnold had his harmonious domestic, and
his laborious official career: Gray, his flowers and his
friendships, his cultured correspondence and his sober
academic home-from-home. But, whereas Gray discovered
in his reflections a source of pure poetry, Arnold for the
most part merely *reflected*, cogitating rather than creating,
beautifully mirroring rather than transforming. Gray's
influence on the younger poet, at times diffused, is at times
extremely obvious; and, when it is most apparent, Gray
benefits by the comparison, while Arnold loses half his
charm. *To a Gipsy Child by the Seashore*, written in 1849,
at once recalls Gray's ode, *On a Distant Prospect:*

> *The Guide of our dark steps a triple veil*
> *Betwixt our senses and our sorrow keeps:*
> *Hath sown with cloudless passages the tale*
> *Of grief, and eas'd us with a thousand sleeps.*
> *Ah! not the nectarous poppy lovers use,*
> *Not daily labour's dull, Lethean spring,*
> *Oblivion in lost angels can infuse*
> *Of the soil'd glory and the trailing wing . . .*

But how much more strongly flows Gray's verse, how much
less turbid is its eloquence! And, where Arnold seems
directly inspired by Gray, and the vision of the Eagle in the
Progress of Poesy:

> *. . . Thy magic lulls the feathered king*
> *With ruffled plumes and flagging wing:*
> *Quench'd in dark clouds of slumber lie*
> *The terror of his beak, and lightnings of his eye*

becomes a Pre-Raphaelite glimpse of the bird of Jove:

> *And the Eagle, at the beck*
> *Of the appeasing gracious harmony,*
> *Droops all his sheeny, brown, deep-feather'd neck,*
> *Nestling nearer to Jove's feet:*
> *While o'er his sovereign eye*
> *The curtains of the blue films slowly meet . . .*

we perceive once again what the decline of the classical ideal had meant to English literature. Every detail that Arnold supplies seems to involve some loss of strength and sharpness. His vividness is the vividness of prose. The nice piece of observation with which he points his last line does not produce that sense of imaginative illumination which is one of the chiefest gifts of poetry.

Some of Arnold's faults are the faults of his age: others appear to be derived from his individual shortcomings, and to denote a sensibility which, although naturally acute, was also oddly intermittent. Of his shortcomings he was himself aware. The real reason, he wrote to his sister, why she found it impossible to enjoy all his poems equally was that " my poems are fragments—i.e., that I am fragments, while you are a whole; the whole effect of my poems is vague and indeterminate. . . ." Yes, his work is remarkably uneven. Here and there it is uncommonly bad—not bad, however, with the positive obstreperous badness of a Wordsworth or a Shelley, whose vices cry to heaven as loudly as their virtues, but with a negative badness, an inward emptiness and deadness. Then his verse becomes sententious and awkward:

> *Like children bathing on the shore,*
> *Buried a wave beneath,*
> *The second wave succeeds, before*
> *We have had time to breathe.*

or, as in *The Strayed Reveller*, laboriously matter-of-fact:

> *They see the Scythian*
> *On the wide Stepp, unharnessing*
> *His wheel'd house at noon.*
> *He tethers his beast down, and makes his meal,*
> *Mares' milk, and bread*
> *Bak'd on the embers:—all around*
> *The boundless waving grass-plains stretch, thick-starr'd*
> *With saffron and the yellow hollyhock*
> *And flag-leav'd iris flowers.*

Here the reader who deprecates investigation into the personal lives of great men may ask himself whether we should not understand Arnold's talent more readily if we knew something of the mysterious early experience that produced the " Marguerite " poems. Whoever she was, whatever she gave, this unknown Frenchwoman, whom he met and loved in Switzerland, left behind her a poignant regret, a mood of nostalgia that coloured all his lyric verse. Loss and separation became dominant themes. Assuming that he had sighed as a lover, it is also clear that, even in Switzerland, he obeyed the call of Rugby. He submitted, but with passionate reservations; and those reservations contributed to the shaping of his whole poetic output. Arnold's position was not exceptional. We think of the Victorian Age as one of strenuous effort, of vigorous belief and of vigorous disbelief. Yet the most notable poems of the period are pitched in quite a different key; and Tennyson and Arnold are at their best, not when they gird up their loins to wrestle with an angel, but when, with a sigh of pagan despondency, they lie down among the Lotus Eaters. Their inclinations may be didactic; their masterpieces are elegiac. Their fortitude does not always impress, but their sensuous melancholy haunts us. *The Scholar Gipsy* and *Thyrsis* are elegies; and Arnold's most successful short poem, *Dover Beach*, begins and ends in lamentation:

> *Listen! you hear the grating roar*
> *Of pebbles which the waves suck back, and fling,*
> *At their return, up the high strand,*
> *Begin, and cease, and then again begin,*
> *With tremulous cadence slow, and bring*
> *The eternal note of sadness in.*

" The eternal note of sadness," working on a sanguine, generous, compassionate, if not profound, intelligence—there perhaps was the origin of Arnold's individual music. He was not so accomplished an artist as Tennyson; but the quality of his mind was very much more interesting. Tennyson interred his inward conflicts beneath a literary monument: Arnold's monument was fragmentary, but he never lost that tremor of youthful awareness, that susceptibility to exquisite pleasures and pains, which Tennyson, so far as we can judge, had by middle age discarded. Thus he remained disconcertingly young in a century which, as he watched, grew dull and old and self-complacent. He was half a pagan—but a pagan with spiritual leanings—in a world whose materialism had assumed the disguise of Christian orthodoxy. A pilgrim like his Scholar Gipsy, he was no more to be subdued or changed by circumstances than Glanvil's fabled wanderer—

> *Still nursing the unconquerable hope,*
> *Still clutching the inviolable shade,*
> *With a free onward impulse brushing through,*
> *By night, the silver'd branches of the glade—*
> *Far on the forest skirts, where none pursue . . .*

93

Spiritual certainty was, no doubt, his goal; but it was not a condition he expected to achieve; and meanwhile the fascination of his pursuit was its apparent fruitlessness. There were consolations in the existence of the unfriended Scholar Gipsy not to be discovered in the organised excitement of any modern crusade.

Edward Lear

THERE IS an important book still to be written about the great Victorian fantasts—a book that, besides tracing their connection with the past and with the reports of other travellers through the universal dream-world, would seek to determine the qualities they shared, and the origin of those qualities both in their personal characteristics and in their literary and social period. Among artists and writers to be discussed, one thinks immediately of Richard Doyle, a draughtsman of fantastic exuberance, whose executive ability was matched by his imaginative oddity: of Lewis Carroll, alias Dodgson, who seems " curiouser and curiouser " the more attentively we contemplate him: and of Edward Lear, a melancholy gadabout, dreaming and grumbling his way through life with Old Foss, his cat, and Georgio Kokali, his devoted Albanian servant. In many respects strikingly dissimilar, they bear, nevertheless, a decided family resemblance. Each was a celibate. Doyle's aversion from marriage is said to have been due to his romantic attachment to a beautiful young married woman, of exemplary virtue and exalted wordly station, from whom he parted, after confessing his love and ascertaining that it was not unreturned, with a mutual determination that they must never meet again. Subsequently Doyle developed a strain of militant Catholic puritanism; and in contrast to the gaiety of his drawings

was his refusal to illustrate *Gulliver's Travels* (which, no
doubt, he would have done admirably) because he considered it an indecent and irreligious volume. The eccentricities of Lewis Carroll—even in Oxford and at a time when
donnish eccentricity was by no means disapproved of—
caused surprise among his circle of friends; for, although
the Victorians, maybe quite rightly, saw no harm in an
unmarried clergyman surrounding himself with attractive
little girls, and passing his leisure hours like the blameless
Grand Turk of an innocent seraglio, the energy with which
he flung himself into their pursuits proved often somewhat
disconcerting. His acquaintances were taken aback when
they entered his rooms to find them apparently deserted, and
then watched him emerge from beneath the table, on all
fours, playing bears or wolves, his little favourites gam-
bolling round him.

His emotional bias was obviously peculiar; and it is
recorded of Lewis Carroll that, as soon as the children he
loved showed signs of maturity, he was apt at once to drop
them. Edward Lear, by comparison, was a sociable and
bustling extrovert. A lover of children, he was also a man of
the world, travelled widely, worked indefatigably, and made
many adult friends with whom he kept up a lively correspondence. But, in spite of his sociability and his extraordinary gift for work—during a six months' tour of India he
sent home no fewer than five hundred and sixty drawings,
nine small sketch books and four journals—his character,
too, had its mysterious and tormented side. He was an
epileptic and suffered, moreover, from chronic asthma and
bronchitis. Though he secured a fair share of its sunshine,
he would appear never to have been quite at home, quite at
his ease, in the world in which he found himself. Life—the
ordinary conditions of day-to-day existence—presented
problems that he could neither ignore nor solve, an abund-

ance of rubs and irritations that he could never learn to take for granted. There was the problem of marriage, the troublesome enigma of the relation of the sexes. . . . " We have no evidence," writes Mr. Holbrook Jackson in his lucid and informative preface to Lear's *Complete Nonsense*,[1] " that he was attracted to women except as friends, and his works, literary and graphic, are as sexless as the artistic efforts of a child." But we must assume that his relative insensibility often slightly disappointed him; and he was inclined to worry about his possible losses and, perhaps rather overemphatically, count his blessings as a celibate, reflecting that were he married he would paint " less and less well " and declaring that the mere thought of " annual infants " drove him nearly frantic. Yet conceivably there *was* something to be said (it struck him once in Corfu) for marriage to a " clever good nice fat little Greek girl," who had " 25 olive trees, some goats and a house." As fate willed it, " the above girl, happily for herself, likes somebody else"; and Lear slipped back into his accustomed round, and into the state of benign perplexity and jocose irascibility that seemed his natural element.

His protests, it is true, were vehement and incessant; but they were almost always tempered with humour—or softened by facetiousness—and delivered in a form that reflected as much upon himself as on the condition of the universe. Noise infuriated him. Thus, in Rome, besides being provoked to frenzy by Manning's " most atrocious sermons," he was reduced to distraction by an odious operatic neighbour, " a vile beastly rottenheaded fool-begotten pernicious priggish screaming, tearing, roaring, perplexing, splitmecrackle, crachimecriggle insane ass of a woman . . . practising howling downstairs with a brute of a

---

[1] *The Complete Nonsense of Edward Lear.* Edited by Holbrook Jackson. Faber.

singing master so horribly, that my head is nearly off." In Switzerland, the children at the hotel, " forty ill-conducted little beasts," caused him to curse the species; while in Paris he complained of the cats—though for cats, at least as personified in Old Foss, he had the utmost veneration— " four hundred and seventy-three . . . making an infernal row in the garden close to my window." But it was to his own character that he eventually returned: he was a " queer beast," he remarked, an " asinine beetle," and he could not understand why so many friends tolerated him. This self-deprecatory refrain creeps into his nonsense verse. In all the best of those incomparable productions, there presently emerges an uncouth and lonely figure—a Dong or a Pobble or a Yonghy-Bonghy-Bo—who strays across the dream-landscape with an air of romantic disenchantment, bound on some endless quest or impelled by the recollection of some mysterious sorrow:

> *And now each night, and all night long,*
> *Over those plains still roams the Dong;*
> *And above the wail of the Chimp and Snipe*
> *You may hear the squeak of his plaintive pipe . . .*
> *And all who watch at the midnight hour,*
> *From Hall or Terrace, or lofty Tower,*
> *Cry, as they trace the Meteor bright,*
> *Moving along through the dreary night,*
> *" This is the hour when forth he goes,*
> *The Dong with a luminous Nose!*
> *Yonder—over the plain he goes;*
> *He goes!*
> *He goes;*
> *The Dong with a luminous Nose! "*

It is difficult to avoid the conclusion that this figure is Lear himself, or bears the same relation to Lear that Childe

Harold bore to Byron, a symbol of his disillusionment, a projection of his own interior restlessness. Among the poems that I personally enjoy most, there is only one on which the romantic shadow does not fall. Uncle Arly comes to a lugubrious end; the Pobble's excursion terminates in disaster; and Yonghy-Bonghy-Bo, irremediably crossed in love, bids a Byronic farewell to the pleasant coast he had inhabited:

> *Down the slippery slopes of Myrtle,*
> *Where the early pumpkins blow,*
> *To the calm and silent sea*
> *Fled the Yonghy-Bonghy-Bo.*
> *There, beyond the Bay of Gurtle,*
> *Lay a large and lively Turtle;*
> *' You're the Cove,' he said, ' for me.*
> *' On your back beyond the sea,*
> *' Turtle, you shall carry me! '*
> *Said the Yonghy-Bonghy-Bo,*
> *Said the Yonghy-Bonghy-Bo.*

The Owl and the Pussy-Cat provide a lyrical exception. Their journey alone—a journey is usually hinted at or described in Edward Lear's poems: he was himself an inveterate traveller, and incurably explorative—winds up with lover's meeting and with the marriage of true minds, as the ill-assorted yet harmonious pair dance hand-in-hand down a shimmering beach beneath the tropic moonlight. Otherwise the note of frustration prevails—attenuated and subtilised by the climate of the dream-world, yet none the less perceptible; for our waking thoughts are bound to invade our dreams, and there is no lasting escape, even in fantasy, from the painful stresses and strains of everyday experience.

Fantasy, that is to say, must remain anchored to reality;

99

and, whereas the haphazard experimentation of Surrealist writers and painters have shown how tediously insignificant may be the results of undirected and uncensored dreaming, we notice that the greatest masters of Victorian fantasy (to some of whom the Surrealists themselves have paid a patronising tribute) combined imaginative hardihood with a considerable inheritance of intellectual discipline. Doyle, like Grandville, was a commercial draughtsman; Carroll, a mathematician; and Lear, a hard-worked topographical and zoological illustrator. Carroll's philosophical and mathematical interests appear, though briefly and fleetingly, both in *Alice's Adventures in Wonderland* and *Through the Looking-Glass*; and Lear's exploration of the miraculous universe of plants and birds and animals gives his imaginary *flora* and *fauna* a remarkable air of accuracy and verisimilitude. It is by his verses that Edward Lear will always be remembered, for nowhere else does the peculiar quality of his imagination—mocking yet plaintive, ludicrous yet elegiac—reveal itself so clearly; but among his most fascinating products is his *Nonsense Botany*. For some tastes it may be a little too whimsical; but the whimsicality of the effect is redeemed by its breath-taking extravagance. One is reminded of Bosch or Breughel, of witches' sabbaths and Temptations of St. Anthony, in which *homunculi* creep out of eggs, half-human fishes crawl with legs on dry land, and sinister domestic utensils peer with glassy orbs from crevices. The inspiration is the same. How strangely different the handling of it! The moral influence of the Victorian age, disinfecting, refining, has extended even to the land of nightmares; yet the innocence of the symbolism and the prosaic neatness of the draughtsmanship make Lear's botanical specimens still more odd and terrifying. A plant blossoms in a slug, the *Sophtsluggia Glutinosa*. Delicate stems are garlanded with boots and shoes, or burst into pigs

GEORGE BRYAN BRUMMELL
by Robert Dighton, 1805

and fiddles, blue-bottles, combs, knives and forks, buns, tea-kettles and barking dogs. *Pollybirdia Singularis* (of which the petals are formed of five impassive parakeets), *Cockatooca Superba* and *Manypeeplia Upsidownia* are exotics that would not be out of place in the man-eating vegetation of an Amazonian jungle.

I have suggested that the figure of Lear himself haunts his own mythology—the Mr. Lear whom it was " pleasant to know " (or so he was inclined to hope), with his spectacles and his bushy beard and his loud and grumbling prejudices, the eccentric bachelor who pottered around San Remo wearing a white mackintosh, pursued by derisive Italian children who imagined that the crazy old Englishman had come out in his nightgown. Certainly his sense of the strangeness of life (which he could scarcely hope to express in the meticulous representation of foreign birds and landscapes) escaped and overflowed into his nonsense verse and pictures; and it was the mixture of adult perplexity and childish sensibility that gave his imaginative escapades their special grace and brilliance. Always a wanderer, never entirely happy, he was disposed to think of contentment as a " loathsome slimy humbug—fit only for potatoes, very fat hogs—and fools generally. Let us pray fervently (he wrote) that we may never become such asses as to be contented." But, although the gift of happiness eluded him, he had possessions of far greater value—the faculty of wonder and the innocent eye of youth. They continued to sustain and enlighten him during the whole course of his long and rambling pilgrimage.

Coventry Patmore

ACCORDING TO a story which I suspect to be apocryphal, but which, since it has always entertained me, I hesitate to disbelieve, the late Roger Fry, that most delightful of men, was once informed by certain friends that, if he had never read the Bible, he really ought to do so. He agreed that he would make the attempt—for Roger Fry, among his numerous virtues, was extremely open-minded—and was later discovered lying on his bed, periodically convulsed by tempests of amusement. Holy Writ had surpassed his expectations; and peal after peal of deep Bloomsburian laughter reverberated round his bedroom walls. " Ha! Ha! Ha! " he kept ejaculating, " *Simply—Too—Extraordinary!* " . . . Fry's attitude towards the Bible was reflected by the attitude of his associates towards widely different questions —by Lytton Strachey, for example, who attacked the whole subject of Victorianism in the same not unfriendly, but cheerfully incredulous, spirit. The entire epoch had been " too extraordinary "—its religious faiths, its social customs, its sentimental reverses, its matrimonial mishaps. More recently, with the gradual decline of Lytton Strachey's influence, a succession of biographers has emerged, doggedly determined to give back to eminent Victorians the qualities that he denied them. It is even suggested that the difficulties under which we supposed they laboured are very largely of our own invention: that they were as estimable, well-balanced and level-headed an assemblage as they themselves imagined. Thus the indefatigable Mr. Hector Bolitho continues to make a courtier-like leg to the majestic shade of Queen Victoria, while Mr. Roger Fulford endeavours to replace her Consort upon his badly shaken pedestal.

Neither attitude will bear examination. The Victorians, though evidently less fantastic and preposterous than Lytton Strachey sometimes sought to show, were also far more extraordinary, far more remote from the present age in all their thoughts and doings, than is dreamed of by biographers who wish to deal a counter-stroke. We have less in common with our Victorian grandparents than with not a few personages of the later eighteenth century; for, much as we may admire the material results they achieved, we no longer breathe the same pervasive moral atmosphere. That atmosphere would be hard to define; but in those who lived through the mid-Victorian age it produced very often an overwhelming sense of tension and anxiety. Such a sense of strain, in some instances stimulating and uplifting, proved in many others exhausting and demoralising. Weak natures were inclined to collapse beneath it; and, in considering any Victorian writer, we must make ample allowance for this disturbing element. Certainly we cannot afford to discount it when we are scrutinising Coventry Patmore, the laureate of Victorian married love and the most ambitious devotional poet of nineteenth-century England. Had his verses been devoid of literary merit, Patmore's life would still provide the basis of a fascinating personal study. He gave to the peculiarities of his age a strongly individual twist, and shaped himself, by dint of his literary talent, into one of the strangest of its famous men.

Born on July 23rd, 1823, he was the son of Peter George

103

Patmore, an associate of Hazlitt and Charles Lamb, and of
his wife, Elizabeth Robertson, a woman of Scottish descent,
who set out to reform her dandified husband, and who
disciplined her children with Presbyterian firmness. Under
her rule Coventry grew up chaste, conscientious, hard-
working. He shunned the example of his somewhat
Micawberish father; but there was that in his temperament
which even his mother's tuition could not quite eliminate.
His amorous passions were unusually strong: ideas of love
and the allurements of the flesh continually pursued him:
and these preoccupations were the cause of many painful
heart-searchings. Since it is better to marry than to burn,
Patmore became engaged and adventured into marriage at
the very earliest opportunity, thereby achieving a degree of
happiness that for the next sixteen years continued to
astonish him; and beneath the mild beams of Emily Patmore's devotion he embarked upon his lifework. It was to
be a glorification of the beauties of married love: an
identification of the link between man and woman with the
relationship between the Soul and God. If Coventry Patmore had at any time been alarmed by pagan stirrings, here
was a philosophy of licensed satisfaction to set his heart and
mind at rest.

The Angel in the House, the poetic expression of his con-
jugal philosophy, began to appear during the year 1854.
Once an immensely popular volume, eagerly discussed on
both sides of the Atlantic, how many adherents can it claim
among modern English readers? That it is minor verse we
can scarcely deny. But few minor poets are so distinctive,
so consistent in their design, on the whole so skilful. Patmore is completely absorbed by his theme; and from an
opening poem, entitled " The Poet's Confidence," in which
with a seraphic absence of false modesty he sets forth what
he means to do—

The richest realm of all the earth
Is counted still a heathen land:
Lo, I, like Joshua, now go forth
To give it into Israel's hand . . .

he proceeds to review the Promised Land by means of a
long series of crisp Victorian vignettes. We enter a cathedral
close—

Geranium, lychnis, rose array'd
The windows, all wide open thrown;
And some one in the Study play'd
The Wedding-March of Mendelssohn.

—breakfast and dine and hear a proposal of marriage, picnic
at Stonehenge, attend Morning Service and re-live the
agonies of a railway-station farewell:

I stood by Honor and the Dean,
They seated in the London train.
A month from her! yet this had been,
Ere now without such bitter pain . . .
The bell rang, and, with shrieks like death,
Link catching link, the long array,
With ponderous pulse and fiery breath,
Proud of its burthen, swept away.

When a poet becomes the prophet of marriage, it is
natural that the biographer should be tempted to investigate
his own matrimonial record. Patmore's first marriage was
exceedingly happy, in so far as he would seem to have loved
his wife with an intense and resolutely faithful, if self-
centred and possessive, ardour. His children, on the other
hand, were very much less fortunate. Patmore and Pontifex
had something in common; and Milnes, his eldest son, a
high-spirited boy, " without a particle of vice " in him, but

with a lamentable propensity towards untidiness and mischief, under the pressure of parental badgering developed at length into a downright rebel. Even the mother's last illness became a weapon in the father's hands; and Tennyson, the second son, who, though more tractable than his brother, Milnes, was not doing quite so brilliantly at Christ's Hospital as his parents had expected, was once the recipient of this appalling message: "I write to remind you (began the anxious patriarch) of your promise to work hard and regain your place at the upper part of your class. . . . Remember, my dear little boy, that you are not likely to have your poor Mama long. Although she does not look very ill, she is really much worse than she was a year ago, and she is *sure* not to live very long. So you should make the best of the time you have to please her."

Emily Honoria, the poet's favourite daughter, who after her mother's death in 1863 made gallant and pathetic attempts to fill the Angel's vacant place, at last, after excruciating inward struggles, retreated to a convent, where she professed a fervid personal cult of the Divine Bridegroom, eventually dying of consumption at the age of twenty-eight. It may be that she had loved her father too deeply; certainly the affection with which he surrounded her had neither soothed or stabilised. "Can that be love," demanded William Blake, "that drinks another as a sponge drinks water?"

The first stage of the poet's career closed at Emily Patmore's death-bed. His wife had left him (Patmore was to complain) with an abruptness and a lack of ceremony that seemed almost inconsiderate:

> *Do you, that have nought other to lament,*
> *Never, my Love, repent*
> *Of how, that July afternoon,*

Coventry Patmore

You went with sudden, unintelligible phrase,
And frighten'd eye,
Upon your journey of so many days
Without a single kiss, or a goodbye? . . .
'Twas all unlike your great and gracious ways.

Put *Departure* beside Bishop King's superb *Exequy*; and not only the thinness of the versification, but the sublime egotism of Patmore's complaint—that his wife had presumed to die, hurriedly, painfully, without the expected and touching farewells—becomes more than ever obvious. It is the kind of grief that fails to arouse sympathy, because it has its roots in no profound or impersonal stratum of feeling, but slips out fluent and exuberant like Patmore's verse.

Mrs. Patmore expired with a sudden flash of prophetic insight; for, as soon as she had gone, she remarked sadly, she knew the priests would get him; and get him they did, about the time he found his second wife, a Catholic lady in comfortable circumstances, whose quiet attachment helped to relieve his sorrow, and whose fortune enabled him to become the master of a roomy Sussex country house. There he initiated a new poetic period. Beside the wild raptures of *The Unknown Eros*, the domestic jubilation of *The Angel in the House* sounds tepid and conventional. With the advance of age, Coventry Patmore did not desist from his researches into the curiously involved origins of heavenly and earthly love. No clue was neglected; and we are informed that a complete collection of the publications of the *Eroticon Biblion Society* was accommodated—though unobtrusively—among his other reference-books. He made full use of the hints they provided, till his admirers, among them Gerard Manley Hopkins, felt now and then that he might be approaching a highly dangerous border-line. The modern critic, whatever his faith and morals, is obliged to

107

admit that their fears were sometimes justified. Crashaw had been reserved by comparison:

> *In all I thee obey! And thus I know*
> *That all is well:*
> *Should'st thou me tell*
> *Out of thy warm caress to go*
> *And roll my body in the biting snow,*
> *My very body's joy were but increased;*
> *More pleasant 'tis to please thee than be pleased . . .*
> *Kiss, tread me under foot, cherish or beat,*
> *Sheathe in my heart sharp pain up to the hilt,*
> *Invent what else were most perversely sweet;*
> *Nay, let the Fiend drag me through dens of guilt;*
> *Let Earth, Heav'n, Hell*
> *'Gainst my content combine;*
> *What could make nought the touch that made thee mine!*

It is easy to be malicious at the expense of the Victorians: it is less easy to understand the strange combination of innocence and experience, of obliquity and clear-sighted vision, of moral hardness and romantic sentimentalism, so often apparent in the conduct of their private lives. Coventry Patmore was an exacting moralist; he was at the same time an exuberant egotist, who seized what he had set his mind on with unselfconscious gusto. His wounds were deep, but they did not fail to heal: his sorrows numerous and genuine, but quickly put behind him or assimilated into literature. The second Mrs. Patmore went the way of the first: a third consoler appeared in the person of his daughter's governess, an attractive and shrewd young person said to have displayed some of the characteristics of the juvenile Becky Sharp. But Eros had not yet done with the poet; and, when he had reached his seventh decade, a final ecstatic love swept down on him. To Alice Meynell he gave the passion of a youth

COVENTRY PATMORE
by John Sargent, 1894

of twenty; but the cool and irreproachable poetess did not
for long appreciate his erotic idealism; and Patmore's
position at her foot-stool was after a while annexed by
Meredith. Alone and palely loitering at the age of seventy-
three, he caught cold during a solitary nocturnal walk and
died on November 26th, 1896. " What about going to
Heaven this time? " were among the poet's last words.

Algernon Charles Swinburne

THE REPUTATION of Villiers de l'Isle-Adam has nowadays fallen into undeserved obscurity. I doubt whether *Contes Cruels*, that admirable collection of short stories, is very often opened; while *Histoires Insolites*, a subsequent collection, is now almost unobtainable. Yet the latter volume, besides *Les Delices d'une Bonne Oeuvre*, an exquisite essay in sardonic low comedy, includes a tale that, although its literary qualities are unimpressive, should be of great interest to every student of nineteenth-century English verse. Entitled *Le Sadisme Anglais*, it describes a conversation between the narrator, an inquiring Gallic journalist, and "*deux jeunes et celèbres littérateurs anglais.*" Villiers' story was published in 1888, not long after the appearance of Stead's notorious articles on the London "white-slave traffic"; and the young Englishmen take up the same theme, deriding the limitations of French debauchery— "*vos trop futiles plaisirs*"—and vaunting the immense superiority of its modern English counterpart. They speak at length, with lingering appreciation: "*Ils s'étendirent en savantes variations sur le viol et sur les moyens dont on se sert, là-bas, pour l'accomplir commodément, soit en certaines demeures de Londres, soit en certains vieux châteaux anglais perdus dans les brumes. Chambres matelassées, oubliettes perfectionnés, anesthésiques et voitures de sûreté défilèrent sur leurs langues*

110

avec une verve sinistre qui eût confondu Ann Radcliff. C'était par milliers et par milliers qu'ils évoquaient les victimes de l' hypocrite lubricité de leurs compatriotes. . . ." The temperament of a people, they add, is reflected by its national poets; and, whereas France has Victor Hugo, " *dont les oeuvres crèvent de santé, de morale convenue et de solonnelles vieilleries,*" England is proud to possess Algernon Charles Swinburne. Warming to their subject, the young men proceed to translate some thirty or forty lines taken from *Anactoria,* with results that are both surprising and slightly dis-concerting; for the comparative bleakness of French prose reveals much that passes largely unnoticed in Swinburne's surging couplets. Images stand out in naked relief, em-phasising the strange emotional distortions of the intellect that produced them.

Such are the revelations, and such the misconceptions, that may overtake the imaginative critic who seeks to understand a foreign work of literature! It would be interesting to know how a copy of *Poems & Ballads* (first printed in 1866) came to Villiers' notice, and whether the two sadistic Englishmen—is it possible that one of them was the young Oscar Wilde, exercising a capricious love of fantasy?—had any real existence. But the episode is grossly misdated; since in 1888—and, as Stead's articles to which the story refers did not appear till 1885, it cannot have been written more than three years earlier—Swinburne for nearly a decade had been safely lodged at Putney, a very decent little literary gentleman of regular and abstemious habits, trotting out on his daily walk to enjoy a single glass of beer, trotting rapidly home to " The Pines," only pausing to pat the head of some attractive infant. The scandal roused by his early works had long ago evaporated; his present pro-ductions were completely blameless; and many of the " unhealthy " enthusiasms of his youth were publicly

discarded under the influence of Theodore Watts-Dunton.
In 1887 he had renounced Whitman; and in 1888 he was
persuaded by Watts to snap the link with Whistler. His
essay, *Mr. Whistler's Lecture on Art*, was an attack on the
doctrine of Art for Art's sake and the whole system of
aesthetic beliefs of which he had once been a devout
adherent. Watts was delighted: Gosse aggrieved: and
Whistler roused to immediate and effective rebuke in a
brief but stinging diatribe, which marked the end of a
valuable intimacy and planted a tombstone, neatly lettered,
upon the grave of Swinburne's talent: " I have lost a
confrère and gained an acquaintance, one Algernon Charles
Swinburne, outsider, Putney."

The relationship of the earlier to the later Swinburne—
of the demonic juvenile adventurer, who startled Mau-
passant, beguiled Ruskin and at the age of twenty-five was
described by Henry Adams as " tropical bird, high-crested,
long-beaked, quick moving, with rapid utterance and screams
of humour . . . a crimson macaw among owls," to the dim
perambulator of Putney Heath, whose public pronounce-
ments often disclosed a streak of ugly chauvinism—has
interested and baffled numerous literary analysts. Gosse
assumed the almost superhuman task of describing his hero's
development, and at the same time avoiding any explicit
reference to the oddities of the constitution in which his
gifts were rooted. Swinburne's alcoholism was lightly
glossed over, while complementary vagaries were allowed
to go unmentioned. We are back again at the old problem
of how far an artist's private career legitimately concerns us.
And of Swinburne it is certainly true that, unless we know
something of his life—a great deal more than Gosse, who
usually played for safety, could bring himself to let slip—
we cannot grasp the true nature of his poetic talent. That
talent was a rich, yet infertile, growth, like the desert aloe

or cactus suddenly throwing out a splendid spire of blossoms, which rapidly declines and decays, as if exhausted by its riotous thrust. The poet's extravagances of conduct were an inseparable part of his creative evolution. He did not write good verse because he drank immoderately, nor did he cease to write memorable poems because his health and nerves were shattered, or because pale ale is less suited to the creation of works of literature than midnight draughts of fiery spirit. But, just as in writing he felt obliged to follow a course of furious self-expenditure and continued to drive his imagination so long as imagination lasted, in life, too, his *daimon* impelled him to squander health and energy, till he sank at length into complete collapse and Watts-Dunton, who had been biding his time, called at Great James Street to remove a helpless stretcher-case.

Undoubtedly he rescued Swinburne from death; and, inasmuch as Swinburne was able to enjoy the twilit existence to which his officious friend restored him, looking forward to his morning glass of ale and to his daily perusal of some little-known Elizabethan or Jacobean drama, the job was worth performing. But Swinburne's imagination was already dead. Indeed it had been moribund some years before the rescue, and the physical collapse followed, rather than preceded, his imaginative bankruptcy. His main period of growth would seem to have taken place between 1860, when he was at work on *Chastelard*, and 1872, when, in his latest biographer's phrase, the death of his revered master Mazzini cast him " rudderless upon the sombre and chaotic seas of his own perverse and fluid temperament."[1] Yet earlier the publication of *Songs Before Sunrise* had shown a gradual falling-off; for Swinburne's generous efforts to play the poetic revolutionary, fulminating against priests and kings and proclaiming the dawn of freedom across benighted

[1]*Swinburne: A Biographical Approach.* By Humphrey Hare. Witherby.

Europe, are somwhat clumsy and artificial compared with the wild rhapsodies of *Poems & Ballads* and *Atalanta in Calydon*. His utterance was still boldly eloquent; but the same intensity of feeling no longer burned behind it. That intensity had a secret and personal origin: it was linked to —if not necessarily derived from—the poet's attitude towards love and his peculiar experience of the commerce of the sexes. " Normal " is, of course, a relative term; but Swinburne was more significantly—one might add, more productively—abnormal than any other modern English writer.

It was Lafourcade who, twenty years ago, first endeavoured to supply the omissions in Gosse's pious portrait, by investigating the temperament that underlay such poems as *The Leper, Faustine, Anactoria*, and emphasising—probably over-emphasising—the part that Richard Monckton Milnes, a renowned collector of erotic books, played in the youthful Swinburne's education. It was not an entirely beneficent part, at least as regards the poet's health and happiness; since Milnes, a hard-headed man of the world and the custodian of one of the richest libraries of " rare and curious " works in Europe—" Oh! how wide is the diapason of my mind," he is said once to have exclaimed, " from what a height to what a depth! "—introduced him to the novels of the Marquis de Sade, the reputation of whose " mystic pages " had already attracted him profoundly. A strange and momentous meeting. Studies that for Houghton were a literary sport, the kind of erudite but amusing diversion that he and his crony Richard Burton had always much delighted in, became for Swinburne a perilous and fascinating journey through the recesses of his own nature. He was an " *excessif,*" as Musset had observed of himself. In his frail and diminutive body, perpetually agitated by nervous twitches, jerks and flutterings, lurked a tempera-

ment that demanded the extremes of emotion and the
constant stimulus of danger—which in one mood caused
him to explore submarine caverns or to swim far out to sea,
disregarding storms and currents: in another, drove him
to brandy and whipped him, when he was drunk, into
epileptic rages. Pain and pleasure were indissolubly connected; images of suffering and cruelty and destruction,
sadistic and masochistic, coloured almost all his early verse.
After a single effort to regain normality—by proposing
marriage in due form to an innocent, thoughtless girl who
laughed at him—he plunged aside into the world of erotic
phantoms—*Félise*, *Faustine* and *Fragoletta*, whose shadowy
company was presently invaded by the solid corporeal shape
of Adah Isaac Menken (christened Dolores Adios McCord),
a booted and spurred *equestrienne* at Astley's Circus. She
was the *Dolores* of a notorious poem and, according to the
existing evidence, probably her lover's only real mistress.

So far the author of *Poems & Ballads* remains a curiosity,
an exhibit for Professor Mario Praz, to be classified with
"the martyred Marquis" (a daring psychological adventurer
but, taken in bulk, an unconscionably boring novelist), the
author of *Venus in Furs* and other insidious exponents of the
pleasure-pain principle. The position that he, in fact, occupies
is immeasurably more important; for, though we cannot discount the strain of perversity and should not pretend that
it was an unfortunate adolescent whim, an eccentric excre-
scence with little bearing on life's work, at his best these
lurid preoccupations were absorbed into his poetic style,
which we must recognise as among the most remarkable
products of late nineteenth-century literature. Often
parodied, he has never been imitated. Nowhere else in the
poetry of his period—neither in the rich and sensuous, yet
lifeless, inventions of Dante Gabriel Rossetti, nor, later, in
the melodious ululations of Ernest Dowson and Lionel

Johnson—do we find such a prodigious surge of vitality, such a cumulative weight of words, bursting with so immediate an effect across the reader's consciousness. Wave follows wave of sound; the wave breaks, the rhythmic hubbub recedes; and then, almost before we have recovered from the confused and thunderous impact, a new toppling roller of sound and fury comes roaring up our mental beach, smothering it with an intricate pattern that shines and coils and melts away. *Mere noise*, an impatient reader protests, usually forgetting his complaint when he succumbs beneath a fresh assault. No one but a man of genius, has remarked T. S. Eliot, " could dwell so exclusively and consistently among words as Swinburne. His language is not, like the language of bad poetry, dead. It is very much alive," with a singular and inimitable life; and the inward life of his language—though the exuberance of Swinburne's style is very often concealing, rather than revealing, witness the extraordinary contrast between the metrical version of *Anactoria* and the translation into French prose—was founded in the last resort on genuine and deep experience, as genuine as the experience which he credited to Charles Baudelaire and sought to describe in *Ave atque Vale:*

> For always thee the fervid languid glories
> Allured of heavier suns in mightier skies;
> Thine ears knew all the wandering watery sighs
> Where the sea sobs round Lesbian promontories,
> The barren kiss of piteous wave to wave
> That knows not where is that Leucadian grave
> Which hides too deep the supreme head of song.
> Ah, salt and sterile as her kisses were,
> The wild sea winds her and the green gulfs bear
> Hither and thither, and vex and work her wrong,
> Blind gods that cannot spare.

As genuine, and yet, one is bound to conclude, in some senses as illusory. For Swinburne the gods are always blind—cruel and mysterious forces, celebrated or reviled but barely half believed in: all loves are barren and tragic: every form of pleasure is ultimately self-destructive. He has none of the breadth of the greatest poets, nothing of that amplitude of human feeling, that majestic variety of tone, which we enjoy in Shakespeare, Milton, Baudelaire (whom Swinburne appreciated exclusively in his most satanic aspect); and a sensible appreciation of his merits was once delivered by John Ruskin. *Atalanta*, he wrote, " in power of imagination and understanding simply sweeps me away . . . as a torrent does a pebble. I'm *righter* than he is—so are the lambs and the swallows, but they're not his match." Poets of the past have been righter—and better: poets of the present day may be righter and more circumspect in their poetic practice. But amid the contemporary chorus of low-voiced twitterings and bleatings, who does not sometimes regret the sonorous confusion of Swinburne's yeasty ocean swell?

The Author of 'Eothen'

KINGLAKE's *Eothen* is one of the most warmly cherished and frequently reprinted of nineteenth-century travel-books; but just why this should be so seems to demand some explanation. The nineteenth century was full of travellers, more romantic, more inquisitive, often far more eloquent. Doughty, Burton, Borrow and Blunt cast larger personal shadows across the landscapes that they rode through; and Doughty and Borrow certainly were more accomplished stylists. Kinglake's line of march has been followed by many other voyagers: his narrative (which was completed after three attempts, and did not appear till nearly ten years after the happenings it dealt with), though it includes a succession of luminous passages, is uneven and fragmentary. The secret of the book's charm, we are bound to conclude, was vested in the author's character. Yet superficially there was nothing very remarkable about the short, energetic, good-humoured young Englishman, fresh from Eton under the rule of Keate and from Trinity College, Cambridge, who in 1834 traversed the Danube with his lively friend Lord Pollington and approached the silent walls of plague-infested Belgrade. His object was the enjoyment of an unconventional holiday. A decade had elapsed since the death of Byron; but in Kinglake's composition lingered some vague Byronic hankerings. He longed to escape from the deadly reign of convention, from the " state of utter respectability " for which his antecedents had prepared him, and to " taste the cold breath of the earliest morn," leading a bright eastern cavalcade " through forests and mountain passes, through deserts and desolate plains," as befitted a spirited youth whose twin passions in childhood had been horsemanship and Homer.

Alexander William Kinglake, however, was no Byron; or perhaps it might be more accurate to say that he was no Childe Harold. If he had a tinge of the poet's romantic restlessness, he had also a fair share of Byron's underlying worldliness; and when the travellers had crossed the ominous border-line dividing a Western from an Eastern empire, and had left behind them the desolate Moslem city —its ruins and narrow windowless lanes, its huge wolfish dogs and heaps of immemorial rubbish, the still air, nevertheless being deliciously laden " with the scent of citron and pomegranate rinds scorched by the sun " and, around the bazaars, " with the dry, dead perfume of strange spices "— they spoke not of Belgrade and the tyranny of the Grand Turk, but of Keate and the Thames and Eton: " we rode along loudly laughing, and talked to the grave Servian forest, as though it were the ' Brocas clump.' " Always ready to be impressed, and capable of recording his impressions in clear and vivid phrases, Kinglake did not feel that by failing to respond to a monument or landscape he had failed to do his duty. He rode up to it, paused to examine the place and, should it arouse no emotional echo, as briskly rode away again. Like Byron, he took " no antiquarian interest in ruins " and quickly tired of sightseeing. He was merely an English gentleman travelling for amusement. The scion of a rich middle-class family, he was destined to practise law as soon as he returned home; and this prospect gave an additional zest to the rôle of wandering milord. Pollington, who was of less resilient stuff, contracted a severe malady and presently threw in his hand. Kinglake went jogging on and on, with his English saddles and his " patent portmanteaus," his tea-cups and his tea-kettle and his jar of Irish butter, still wearing the London hat and waistcoat which earned him savage looks from the fanatical populace of Nablous, but which, characteristically, it did not occur to him to lay aside. Not for Kinglake was disguise or evasion. In Nablous he continued to stroll abroad; and in Damascus he walked on the raised pavement hitherto reserved for the feet of true believers. Luckily, the British consul was a potent personage; and the disciplinary methods of Ibrahim Pasha, who refused to countenance racial persecution, were yet a painful memory. Moreover, Kinglake was evidently a brave man. He had confronted the plague in Belgrade, and had dared it to do its worst in the sand-paved streets of Cairo. A traveller who had witnessed the rages of Keate could endure with equanimity the " fixed glassy looks " of furious Moslem pietists.

The East stirred him, but it did not enslave. London was " the only place for fun," he might have said with Byron, and England the only country, in spite of the horrid conventionalism of English social habits, where existence was firmly based on the values that he recognised. The sight of a fellow Englishman was apt to move him deeply; and in mid-desert, between Gaza and Cairo, he enjoyed a curious chance-meeting. Day after day he had ridden forward through the incandescent sun-haze, listening to the groaning of his Arabs, the plaintive sighing of his camels. Then on the horizon appeared a quivering speck. It drew closer, assumed a definite form:

In a little while we saw that one of the riders wore European dress, and at last the travellers were pronounced to be an English gentleman and his servant; by their side were a couple of Arabs on foot. . . . This Englishman, as I afterwards found, was a military man returning to his country from India. . . . As for me, I had come pretty straight from England, and so here we met in the wilderness about half-way from our respective starting-points. As we approached each other it became with me a question whether we should speak. I thought it likely that the stranger would accost me, and in the event of his doing so, I was quite ready to be . . . sociable . . .; but still I could not think of anything that I had to say to him . . . I was shy and indolent, and I felt no great wish to stop and talk like a morning visitor in the midst of those broad solitudes. The traveller perhaps felt as I did, for except that we lifted our hands to our caps, and waved our arms in courtesy, we passed each other quite as distantly as if we had passed in Pall Mall.

But the Arab attendants were less inhibited. They huddled together in excited converse, and Kinglake's camel herself suddenly " caught the social feeling." Since she declined to proceed, he wheeled her about, and " found that the gallant officer . . . was exactly in the same predicament. . . . He was the first to speak. Too courteous to address me, as if he admitted the possibility of my wishing to accost him from any feeling of mere sociability on civilian-like love of vain talk, he at once attributed my advances to a laudable wish of acquiring statistical information; and accordingly, when we got within speaking distance, he said ' I dare say you wish to know how the plague is going on at Cairo?' . . ."

From this agreeable passage it will be clear that Kinglake lacked neither an appreciation of drama nor a sense of social comedy. The meeting had a pleasantly ludicrous, but also a symbolic, aspect; and one cannot resist the suspicion that its upshot disappointed him. How much more appropriate to have converged and diverged with distant gentlemanly gestures—two Englishmen each in pursuit of the Englishman's historic destiny, each clinging to his traditional reserve, each politely but ever so remotely aware of the other's claim to recognition! Yet, notwithstanding insular quirks, Kinglake's outlook was undimmed by the cruder sort of patriotic prejudice. He had a variety of obvious English failings—a reluctance, for example, to take the faith and civilisation of alien races altogether seriously; but they were accompanied by an assemblage of corresponding virtues. Thus, he was open-minded, independent and sceptical, and felt a genuine contempt for any form of humbug. *Eothen* has been compared to *A Sentimental Journey*: and the comparison, though it may be over-emphasised, has much to recommend it. Both are intensely personal records; both are the work of writers who were concerned with the incidents of travel only in so far as those incidents had made a lasting mark on their own personal sensibility. That sensibility was keen but spasmodic. Sterne and Kinglake were equally attracted to women; and at the touch of sensuous beauty their restive imaginations flared up. Women to Kinglake were the colour and the light of life. Pretty women, of course; for, as he admitted with a frankness or a cynicism unusual in his period, " except when we refer to the beautiful devotion of the mother to her child, all the fine things we think and say about women apply only to those who are tolerably good-looking . . ." The haggard Bedouin women, whom he observed around their squalid tents, " were not within the scope of the privilege . . ." But the Christian maidens of " sweet Bethlehem " afforded an intoxicating spectacle, which pleased and interested him far more than his observation of the Holy Places. At Cairo he passed some happy hours, visiting the slave market and

allowing it to be understood that he wished to buy a con-
cubine—a young Circassian, according to the dealer as
lovely as the full moon, who, once she had emerged from the
mass of white linen in which she was enshrouded, displayed
a " large face perfectly round and perfectly white," but
otherwise without the smallest trace of the promised lunar
fascination. It was at Nazareth, in the so-called home of the
Virgin, that he permitted his voluptuous propensities the
greatest imaginative licence. " Fevered with the zeal of an
insane devotion to the heavenly queen of Christendom," he
forgot the precepts of his sternly Protestant youth, and
acclaimed a religion that bade him " fear God, and be pious,
and yet not cease from loving." He did not hesitate to
perform a perfervid obeisance:

> With a half consciousness—with the semblance of
> a thrilling hope that I was plunging deep, deep into my
> first knowledge of some most holy mystery, or some new,
> rapturous, and daring sin, I knelt, and bowed down my
> face till I met the smooth rock with my lips. One moment
> —one moment—my heart, or some old pagan demon
> within me woke up, and fiercely bounded—my bosom
> was lifted, and swung—as though I had touched her
> warm robe. One moment—one more, and then—the
> fever left me. I rose from my knees. I felt hopelessly
> sane. The mere world reappeared.

The last sentence seems particularly deserving of note.
Always in Kinglake's moods there were these abrupt, unselfconscious returns to everyday existence. He was an amateur
of feelings, just as he was an amateur of travel, and remained,
where *Eothen* is concerned, an amateur in the art of writing.
But there is no doubt that he was an extraordinarily brilliant
amateur. And may it not have been just that shade of wayward amateurishness, coupled with his exquisitely sharp eye

and magnificent descriptive *flair*, which has given him so firm a hold on the affections of his readers, in a country where undue professionalism is often slightly suspect? Beside Kinglake, Doughty is a disturbing phenomenon—a zealot who forces himself to undergo appalling physical hardships, then spends year after laborious year grimly hammering out a prose style. Kinglake enjoyed his travels and, so far as we can judge from his book, he enjoyed the task of chronicling them. Doughty is the humourless professional artist: Kinglake, an itinerant man of the world who, having arisen from his knees, salutes the familiar world around him. The warm robe of the Queen of Heaven has dissolved beneath his finger-tips. We can imagine him brushing his shins, replacing the London hat and smiling at his own enthusiasm, as he rewards the custodian monk and strides back into the sunlight. There was nothing about him of the romantic recluse, the aristocratic defender of lost causes, the visionary exile. His fate was not with Lady Hester Stanhope, dying in exalted solitude among rebellious tribesmen, not with Byron paying a legendary forfeit amid the gloom of Missolonghi. Returning to England as his relations intended, Kinglake took to law and politics, failed as a parliamentary speaker but composed the history of the Crimean War in eight impressive volumes.

Daniel Defoe

IN EVALUATIONS of character by modern novelists, one of
the strongest of human passions has often been neglected.
True, it is not also one of the oldest; for it may be said to
have grown up with modern society and only assumed
its present importance during the last three hundred years.
The Elizabethans and their immediate successors knew very
little of it. In their minds the possibilities of tragic action
were still bounded by a few comparatively simple motives—
—ambition, revenge or sexual appetite; and not until we
have passed the Civil War, and entered a world that
recognisably suggests our own, does the new motive make
its appearance in a work of literature. The passion for
respectability is of recent growth. Yet how real it is, how
lasting, on occasions how destructive! Half the crimes of
passion of the nineteenth and twentieth centuries have had
as their mainspring not passion in the ordinary sexual sense
(which the criminal in most instances has already satisfied)
but the desire to escape from illicit love into respectable
married life. Modern capitalism has created a gigantic class
for whom conformity is synonymous with moral virtue, and
security is the true foundation of personal happiness. Such
a point of view already existed in the pre-Augustan period:
and its prophet was Daniel Defoe, a man sufficiently close to
the life of the people and conversant with the standards of a

struggling *bourgeoisie* to have discovered that, if one exists always on the verge of wretchedness, in the grey half-world that divides the decently prosperous from the completely destitute, certain pretensions become more, rather than less, important, and that the determination to " keep one's end up " socially is an expression of the will to live.

Himself Defoe was a man of enormous energy who experienced considerable changes of fortune; and it is their remarkable vitality that distinguishes all the personages he created—their refusal to be downed by circumstance and the insect-like persistence with which they continue to scheme and shove. Both *Moll Flanders* and *Roxana* have moral endings—virtue is rewarded and vice, somewhat tardily, receives a rap on the knuckles; but in the last analysis each of them is an essentially moral book. No wonder that George Borrow, lounging disconsolately across Westminster Bridge after days spent in wringing a livelihood from the Newgate Calendar (whence he had begun to imbibe " strange doubts . . . about virtue and crime "), was shocked to see a copy of *Moll Flanders*, black, greasy, dog-eared, in the hands of an old apple-woman who sat on the pavement, and to hear her describe its heroine as " the blessed woman." Her darling son, explained the apple-woman, was a transported convict; and through those eyes Moll's acquisitive and combative qualities shone with a lustre that was both unexpected and disconcerting. The protagonist's misdeeds were excused by her success and courage. Her criminal habits were not a psychological eccentricity—the idea of the *acte gratuit* derives from the well-to-do—but had behind them the impetus of a genuine social passion. Besides, Moll Flanders is an extraordinarily English character; and, as we read her story we are reminded, again and again, that England is the country where almost everyone is conscious of being a little better than somebody else. Moll thanks her stars repeatedly that she is not as other sinners; and, although through force of circumstances she lives in the present moment, she is supported by recollections of respectability and by the relics of a good education and a middle-class upbringing. Thank God, she " had been bred up tight and cleanly "! Among the thieves, fences and prostitutes with whom her lot is cast, she never loses sight of her own superior origins; and, when at last she finds herself committed to Newgate, what horrifies her is the indecorous squalor of her new environment: " the hellish noise, the roaring, swearing and clamour, the stench and nastiness. . . ." Later, the fact that most distresses her is that she, too, should so quickly have become acclimatised:

> I had a weight of guilt upon me, enough to sink any creature who had the least power of reflection left . . I had at first some remorse, indeed, but no repentance; I had now neither remorse nor repentance. . . . A certain strange lethargy of soul possessed me. I had no trouble, no apprehensions, no sorrow. . . . The first surprise was gone. . . . I was engulfed in the misery of punishment and had an infamous death at the door; and yet I had no sense of my condition, no thought of heaven or hell, at least that went any farther than a bare flying touch, like the stitch or pain that gives a hint and goes off.

It would be absurd, of course, to pretend that Defoe develops or builds up his heroine's character with the self-conscious artistry of a modern novelist. But, because he understood her so well and delineated her background from first-hand knowledge, the character that does emerge has an astonishing sharpness. Primarily, *Moll Flanders* is an essay in storytelling—written, one imagines, at break-neck speed, with care for the picturesque quality of every episode: but there are few incidents that could be discarded without loss to the whole. Thus, the explanation of Moll's adventures as an adult is provided by a detail of her early youth. She had been a foundling, put out to nurse in the house of a country-woman: and one day her foster-mother, coming into the room " where all the poor children were at work . . . sat down just over against me, not in her usual place as mistress. . . . ' Thou foolish child,' says she, ' thou art always crying.' " The little girl refused to be comforted: whereat—

> She began to be angry with me. . . . Says she . . . " Is the girl mad? What! would you be a gentlewoman? "
>
> " Yes," says I . . .
>
> This set the old gentlewoman a-laughing at me. . . . " Well, madam, forsooth," says she . . . " you would be a gentlewoman; and how will you come to be a gentle-woman? What! will you do it by your fingers' ends? "
>
> " Yes," says I again, very innocently.
>
> " Why, what can you earn? " says she; " what can you get a day at your work? "
>
> " Threepence," says I, " when I spin, and fourpence when I work plain work."
>
> " Alas! poor gentlewoman," said she again, laughing, " what will that do for thee? "

Yet Moll's bold prediction is presently justified. She is adopted by the Mayoress of the town, reared among her daughters and, when she reaches puberty, seduced by the elder son. Here romantic passion, for the first and for the last time, puts in an appearance. He tells her that he loves her; " and my heart spoke as plain as a voice that I liked it." He promises marriage, then breaks his word and suggests that she should marry instead his younger brother. Her reply is magnificent in its plainness and brevity:

> " No, sir," said I, " depend upon it 'tis impossible, and

ALGERNON CHARLES SWINBURNE

whatever the change on your side may be, I will ever be true; and I had much rather, since it is come to that unhappy length, be your whore than your brother's wife."

But Moll Flanders is nothing if not an opportunist. Cynically or philosophically, she decides to give way: and Defoe's summing-up is a masterpiece of ingenious understatement:

> It concerns the story in hand very little to enter into further particulars of the family, or of myself, for the five years that I lived with this husband, only to observe that I had two children by him, and that at the end of the five years he died. . . . I confess I was not suitably affected with the loss of my husband. . . . He was a tender, kind, good-humoured man . . . but his brother being so always in my sight . . . was a continual snare to me; and I never was in bed with my husband, but I wished myself in the arms of his brother. . . . In short, I committed adultery and incest . . . every day in my desires. . . .

To re-read Defoe's narrative with attention is to despair almost of the future of the English language. In detail, there is much that is slipshod; but the general effect is one of accuracy combined with lucidity. The virile prose of the late seventeenth century can hardly be over-praised. It has outgrown the euphuisms of the Elizabethans and has not yet acquired the somewhat ponderous latinistic elegance that it was gradually to take on during the Augustan age. It is a *modern* prose, made to be spoken by modern people, and admirably suited to the description of a world of muddy streets, hackney coaches, shops, warehouses, and hungry, hurrying passers-by. In that world—the universe of commercial London, shadowed by its brownish pall of " sea-coal " fog—there is little room for spiritual airs and graces, abstract speculation or poetic fancy. The men and women

Defoe deals with have always their livings to gain; and his greatest novel faithfully reflects their standards. After her first experience of romantic passion (so nearly fatal), the heroine gives a wide berth to any form of excess or insobriety. She distrusts it in herself: she condemns and despises it when she sees it in others. She may not hesitate to go to bed with a drunken gentleman, rob him during the coach-ride of " a gold watch, with a silk purse full of gold, his fine full-bottom periwig and silver-fringed gloves, his sword and fine snuff-box," allow her " governess," the receiver of stolen goods, to do some quiet blackmailing, then agree to meet him again and become his mistress; but she is horrified nevertheless by his presumption and folly— " there is nothing (she reflects) so absurd, so surfeiting, so ridiculous as a man heated by wine in his head, and a wicked gust in his inclination together. . . ." She has the innate respectability of the typical prostitute.

Put *Moll Flanders* side by side with one of the Goncourts' novels: and the immense superiority of the earlier method becomes apparent. For the Goncourts envisaged *Germinie Lacerteux* (their own maid-of-all-work, whose secret they had happened to discover after her death) from the point of view of privileged dispassionate aesthetes. They look down into her life. Defoe seems to be looking up at us from that life itself—to partake of, and yet transcend, its confusion and drabness. Not for him the elaborate processes of aesthetic eavesdropping by which the French novelists were obliged to refresh their imagination. As he writes, the wheels are thundering along the narrow streets: the kennels swim with mud: the rain-water gurgles in leaden gutters and splashes down on to the pavements of the commercial city. Moll Flanders is any woman carrying a bundle, looking from time to time over her shoulder, hurrying independent yet furtive through fog or rain. The least " imaginative," certainly the least literary, of English writers, Defoe is capable of a simplicity and force and eloquence that any modern novelist is bound to envy, while sudden flashes of imaginative insight redeem his commonplace. And not for a moment does he lose touch with the central drama—the tragedy of the little foundling who would be a gentlewoman and follows a will-o'-wisp of social advancement through the London underworld, pursued by the spectres of degradation and hunger and misery. " It was all fear without, and dark within," she exclaims in a particularly moving passage in which she describes how she was tempted to commit a murder. Elsewhere—it might serve as epigraph to the entire bulky volume: ". . . The terror of approaching poverty lay hard upon my spirits."

'Les Liaisons Dangereuses'

A SNOB is not infrequently a human being who, beneath the public parade of one form of happiness, attempts to conceal the gratification he derives from another. Thus a social snob may pretend that he enjoys parties because he is naturally and incurably gregarious, when in fact they serve to titillate a secret romanticism. The epicurean snob snuffs at vintages or collects fine editions, not so much because he is interested in typography or fond of claret, as because these tastes give him a delightful distinction among his duller acquaintances. A sexual snob (and there are more of them than one might at first suspect) is usually a power-addict disguised as a pleasure-lover. For the study of such a temperament and its various implications we have a brilliant and authoritative text-book in *Les Liaisons Dangereuses*. One of the most original, certainly the most curious, of eighteenth-century novels, Choderlos de Laclos's narrative still enjoys a reputation for prodigious impropriety which is apt to blind a reader to its psychological virtues. Yet few novels with a predominantly sexual theme are less salacious. Though the situations depicted are exceedingly unconventional, and the two chief characters cultivated specimens of extreme depravity, the accent throughout is on the pleasures of the mind rather than on the joys of the body: the protagonists practise seduction in the spirit of virtuosos. Beneath the flurry and

132

heat and palpitation of a passionate love affair, they are in search always of the master-springs of the victim's conduct. What makes the puppet move? Why does it exclaim and writhe? Both M. de Valmont and his counsellor and confederate, Madame de Merteuil, are intelligent, analytical, cold, inquisitive, contemptuous of and yet fascinated by their companions' shortcomings. It is their pride to enjoy but never feel; the perversion they favour is to keep a cool head even in the transports of passion, but at the same time allow their natural passions the fullest licence. Weaker mortals (they have discovered) have not this gift. Each is a snob, an addict of power, obsessed by the consciousness of his or her own personal superiority. Competitive professionals who have formerly been lovers (and might long ago have renewed the tie, were they not deeply and justifiably suspicious of one another's motives), they exchange advice and compliments, snubs and reprimands. Meanwhile, they range like elegant beasts of prey through Parisian high society. . . . But here it must be noted, as an interesting sidelight on the novelist's period, that, although Choderlos de Laclos placed the scene of his story in the capital and adjacent country houses, his subject matter seems to have been gathered from small provincial towns which he visited following his career as a captain of artillery. Not very much is known otherwise of the writer's life. Born at Amiens in 1741, he entered the service at the age of eighteen, achieved the rank of captain in 1778 and afterwards attached himself to the Duc d'Orléans. " *À cette époque* " (we learn) " *il fréquente le monde and il observe.*" No doubt in the entourage of an intriguing Prince of the Blood there was literary material of very unusual interest; and the Captain was an observer of uncommon aptitude. " *C'était un grand monsieur*" (writes Trilly in his *Mémoires pour servir à l'Histoire des Moeurs de la fin du XVIIIe siècle*) " *maigre, jaune, en habit*

noir." Such a portrait—in conjunction with Bailly's pastel:
a broad prominent forehead and sharp eyes under contracted
eyebrows—suits well enough with the idea of the novelist
we have already gathered. Choderlos de Laclos was not
a likeable, but a remarkably perceptive, man—quiet, precise, calculating, perhaps a trifle sinister, who saw a great
deal and forgot nothing and harboured few illusions, but
made up in clarity of insight what he lacked in warmth of
feeling.

His view of love was neither sentimental nor weakly
frivolous. Of that detestable ingredient *le sel gaulois*, his
masterpiece does not include the smallest sprinkling. The
intrigues he describes may not be earnest; but, alike in their
origins and outcome, they are extremely serious, dignified
by grace and skill and deliberate villainy. There is seldom
a smile and never a smirk through the whole extraordinary
narrative. In a sense, Valmont and Madame de Merteuil
are tragic characters. They have the right tragic concentration upon a single issue; this immorality is as definite and
thoroughgoing as art can make it. One hastens to add,
however, that they are not incredible. We may none of us
have known a Madame de Merteuil, as she is presented in
her literary essence by Choderlos de Laclos; but we have
many of us encountered men and women in whom the
consciousness of possessing great attractions, and the
satisfaction of preying on the feelings of others, have
triumphed over all the warmer emotions and less inhuman
instincts. What the sadistic Madame de Merteuil has
learned by painful study she teaches in suffering; and a key-
passage of *Les Liaisons Dangereuses* is the heroine's account
of the education from which she has evolved her talents.
Even as a young girl, she watched and analysed. Even her
wedding-night at sixteen was an experience of which every
moment was noted and recorded:

> *J'attendais avec sécurité le moment qui devoit m'instruire,
> et j'eus besoin de réflexion pour montrer de l'embarras et de
> la crainte. Cette première nuit, dont on se fait pour l'ordinaire
> une idée si cruelle ou si douce, ne me présentoit qu'une occasion
> d'expérience; douleur et plaisir, j'observai tout exactement,
> et ne voyais dans ces diverses sensations, que des faits à
> recueillir et à méditer.*

By comparison, Valmont is almost a bungler. " *Ma belle
amie* " (he confesses, *à propos* of the siege he is laying to
Madame de Tourvel) " *l'homme le plus adroit ne peut encore
que se tenir au niveau de la femme la plus vraie.*" The
relationship between an unscrupulous man and an unscrupulous woman, the instinctive sympathy that unites
Valmont and Madame de Merteuil, and the competitive
antagonism that divides them—there is the real pivot of the
writer's subject. Other characters, though admirably drawn,
are incidental. Madame de Merteuil tries person after
person, and finds them all unworthy. Together with Valmont she exists on a lonely height; and " *en vérité* (remarks
her friend) *plus je vais, et plus je suis tenté de croire qu'il n'y
a que vous et moi dans le monde, qui valions quelque chose.*"
Most potential victims are such easy game as to be quite
uninteresting. Madame de Merteuil's lover Belleroche is a
fool, and his devotion bores her; Prévan is attractive but
a conceited nincompoop, and she has no difficulty in out-
witting and humiliating that talkative seducer. Of Cécile
de Volanges, fresh from the schoolroom, whom she assists in
her prentice love affair with the Chevalier Danceny, the
experienced woman of the world has at first high hopes:

> . . . *elle est vraiment délicieuse! Celà n'a ni caractère ni
> principes: jugez combien sa société sera douce et facile . . .
> sans esprit et sans finesse, elle a pourtant une certaine fausseté*

naturelle, si l'on peut parler ainsi, qui quelquefois m'étonne moi même. . . .

She bends over the child's development as over the flowering of an exotic plant, only to admit some time later that she is gravely disappointed:

> *Je me désintéresse entièrement sur son compte . . . elle dénote, surtout, une faiblesse de caractère presque toujours incurable . . . de sorte que, tandis que nous nous occuperions à former cette petite fille pour l'intrigue, nous n'en ferions qu'une femme facile. Or, je ne connais rien de si plat que cette facilité de bêtise: qui se rend sans savoir ni comment ni pourquoi, uniquement parce qu'on l'attaque et qu'elle ne sait pas résister. Ces sortes de femmes ne sont absolument que des machines a plaisir.*

Valmont, nevertheless, is a man after her own tastes: an immoralist whose behaviour is regulated by a strict personal code:

> *Encore plus faux et dangereux qu'il n'est aimable et séduisant, jamais, depuis sa plus grande jeunesse, il n'a fait un pas ou dit une parole sans avoir un projet . . . sa conduite est le résultat de ses principes. Il sait calculer tout ce qu'un homme peut se permettre d'horreurs sans se compromettre; et pour être cruel et méchant sans danger, il a choisi les femmes pour victimes.*

—a strategist who piques himself on the elegance of his manœuvres: *Jusques-là* (he writes to Madame de Merteuil) *vous me trouverez, je crois, une pureté de méthode qui vous fera plaisir. . . . Jugez-moi donc comme Turenne ou Frédéric.*

Alas, that even Valmont should have human failings! The discovery by Madame de Merteuil of her old friend's weakness—the account, elaborately detailed through a

succession of letters, of how, in the irresistible flashing
course they run side by side, trampling underfoot hearts and
hopes and lives and marriages, Madame de Merteuil begins
gradually to draw ahead, and Valmont, in spite of his
protestations, to flag behind, till one arch-cynic has as good
as admitted that he loves the other—provides the real drama
or true tragedy, of *Les Liaisons Dangereuses*. Laclos's age
was a period of civil war between the heart and brain. It
was the age of Rousseau (from whose *Nouvelle Héloïse*
Valmont and Madame de Merteuil are fond of quoting),
but it was also the age of Voltaire and Voltaire's progeny.
It was tormented by the conflict of sense and sentiment;
and from both sprang the vast upheaval of 1789, with its
sentimental but murderous *doctrinaires*, its poetic patriots,
its massacres and flowery thanksgivings and Feasts of
Reason. A copy of *Les Liaisons Dangereuses*, richly bound,
bearing no title but embossed with the arms of Marie
Antoinette, is preserved on the shelves of the Bibliothèque
Impériale. The novel was first published in 1782; the
novelist died as one of Napoleon's generals. Born among
the fading lilies of royal France, he expired amid the
sphinxes and eagles of a new imperial Europe. Laclos's
decline over laps the youth of Henri Beyle. Together they
are two chief progenitors of the modern novel.

'Le Lys dans la Vallée'

AMONG THE furnishing of the great gloomy house that he planned for Madame Hanska, Balzac was obliged to leave a good many empty spaces. On the naked wall, however, he would inscribe a rectangle, and within the rectangle he would chalk up a scribbled note that this space had been reserved for a canvas by Raphael or Guido Reni. There are casual, though appreciative, readers of the *Comédie Humaine* to whom an expedition through the works of Balzac may have suggested an expedition round that unfinished house. So numerous are the spaces that have not been filled. So often does Balzac, in the excitement and haste of the creative process, merely indicate briefly and crudely what he means to do. So abrupt are the transitions from first- to fifth-rate. It is disconcerting, for example, to move on from the marvellous last chapters of *Les Illusions Perdues* to the wild and clumsy melodrama that comes next in the series. Sinister police spies, ethereal consumptive prostitutes, master criminals of an earthly guile and daring, are sketched in by a *feuilleton*-writer who was also a genius, but had no sense of when he ceased to be one and became the other. A certain insensitiveness is apt to accompany tremendous talent. In Balzac that insensitiveness is frequently stupefying.

It is fortunate that the unexpectedness of Balzac's gifts should have been in direct proportion to their incompleteness. Suddenly we come face to face with *Le Lys dans la Vallée*, a story that—dangerous though it may be to compare two arts so different as writing and painting—recalls a panel picture by some French master of the early Renaissance, given the sentiment and subject-matter of a more troubled age. The effect produced is extraordinarily fresh and clear and brilliant. As in some of his most memorable long short stories, Balzac is content to expend all his genius upon the analysis of a single situation and to allow the interest of that situation to excuse itself. He had reason to feel satisfied when the story was finished. His dedication testifies to the pride he took in it, to the pleasure he derived from its elegant workmanship—so unlike the haphazard workmanship of his other books. No artist was ever less of a dilettante; but he was too genuine an artist not to venerate order, though for the most part he saw order as grandeur, and grandeur as magnitude.

In scale and theme, *Le Lys dans la Vallée* is equally limited. Its story—well, that it shares with half a dozen other excellent French novels; for it is concerned with the protracted passion of a very young man for a virtuous but passionate married woman. Later, Flaubert was to spin out such an episode—with what magnificent results!—into two whole volumes. Fromentin was to base *Dominique* on a similar love-affair. In fact, the subject was the common property of an entire generation which regarded disappointment as the badge of the " high-born " spirit, and remembered and regretted the more keenly when it did not enjoy. But *Le Lys dans la Vallée* has not yet " dated "; and, though characteristically—even delightfully—the work of a period, the narrative also exists on a far less impermanent plane. Apart from his somewhat unfortunate expeditions into downright melodrama, and his generally disastrous flights into the realms of metaphysical speculation, for

Balzac the truly romantic was always the concrete. He loves to situate his personages in a definite place and time, establish their genealogies and fix their incomes. He understands that human beings have two sorts of existence. They have an inner life, but simultaneously they live and express themselves through the material objects—through the houses and furniture and small personal belongings—among which their time is spent. Balzac's " realism " is essentially poetic. It has nothing about it of that dull exhaustive naturalism which appals and overwhelms us in the Goncourts or Zola. He shows us the outer world transfigured and irradiated by its human significance. Thus the little white ancient château on the hillside, with its small symmetrical façade and five windows looking south over the silvery Indre, becomes immediately the expression of its mistress's life—isolated, obscure, modest but beautifully ordered. And then, there is the first glimpse of Madame de Mortsauf's drawing-room, its panelled walls painted in two shades of grey, the white-and-gold porcelain vases on the chimney piece, the white curtains and the drab chair-covers plainly edged with green.

The appearance of M. de Mortsauf is cleverly calculated. Here is a life which, as revealed in its outward equipment, might seem to leave no loophole for discord, unhappiness or moral *malaise*. M. de Mortsauf enters; and the illusion dissolves. Years of life abroad as an *émigré* have broken his spirit. It is true that he is still energetic and industrious; but spiritual vitality and physical health have alike deserted him. He is restless, embittered, remorseful, the uneasy husk of a man, a self-tormenting tyrant who preys on his family:

Agé seulement de quarante-cinq ans, il paraissait approcher de la soixantaine, tant il avait promptement vieilli dans le

*grand naufrage qui termina la 18e siècle. Le demi-couronne,
qui ceignait monastiquement l'arrière de sa tête dégarnie de
cheveux, venait mourir aux oreilles en caressant les tempes par
des touffes grises mélangées de noir. Son visage rassemblait
vaguement à celui d'un loup blanc qui a du sang au museau,
car son nez était enflammé comme celui d'un homme dont la vie
est altérée dans ses principes, dont l'estomac est affaibli, dont
les humeurs sont viciées par d'anciennes maladies. . . . Son
oeil clair, jaune et dur, tombait sur vous comme un rayon en
hiver, lumineux sans chaleur, inquiet sans pensée, défiant sans
objet. Sa bouche était violente et impérieuse, son menton était
droit et long.*

Moreover, the two children, on whom he had placed all his
hopes, have inherited the debility of his constitution; and
the tragedy of life at the château of Clochegourde is implicit
in the contrast between Madame de Mortsauf, young,
healthy, beautiful, and the pinched, impoverished-looking
children—idolised by both parents—whom she owes to her
husband's sufferings and dissipations when he wandered as
a landless exile through the cities of Europe. M. de Mortsauf, who is perpetually aware of the contrast and tortured
by a spectacle he cannot escape, finds relief in increasing
harshness towards the children's mother. The narrator in
the rôle of humble *soupirant* hovers on the verge of this
distracted household.

A story so admirably told does not bear re-telling. Its
charm depends in part on the flow of a simple harmonious
narrative, and the flashes of acute observation by which it
is enlivened: in part on the development and parallel
prolongation of a number of complementary but opposing
themes. Death and life rub shoulders at the château of
Clochegourde; and Madame de Mortsauf, struggling
against the principle of dissolution and decay that she

observes in her children and her husband, expends to no purpose the resources of her strength and beauty. Then, there is the conflict engendered by the narrator's love—a passion equally pure and sensual, devoted and selfish, doomed by its own sterility yet sublime in its uselessness. Platonic love is not the easiest subject for any novelist, since it is the essence of such a love that it should drag on and on, without the relief or contrast afforded by physical love-making. Its history, like its pleasures, remains subjective; but, though Balzac's personages are sometimes irritating, and though from talk they often descend to delivering speeches, they never lose their shape in the imagination. The effect may be a little absurd; but so is passion itself. Madame de Mortsauf is still a woman despite her virtues; and the fact that, at the very end of her blameless life, she should snatch greedily but ineffectually at the idea of happiness, before relapsing into the attitude of conventional piety, helps to illustrate her career of suffering in its true perspective. She, too, had been voluptuous, passionate, fallible. The measure of her moral triumph is the extent of her misery.

The celestial Venus demands an earthly counterpart. Lady Dudley, with whom Félix takes refuge from his idol's exclusive and exhausting platonism, is one of Balzac's most fascinating minor characters—an odd mixture (stirred up to boiling point over the blaze of the novelist's meridional fancy) of the Ladies Hester Stanhope and Caroline Lamb. She is English—and that alone says almost everything; her birthplace is the country of violent extremes, boundless eccentricity, huge fortunes, crumbling ghost-ridden castles, crazy Dukes, green tea, whisky and perpetual fogs. Disturbing ancestral influences seethe through her veins. " *Je suis née le Lancashire* " (she exclaims defiantly)—" *pays où les femmes meurent d'amour* "; and

she has an artistry in the cultivation of material pleasures
that Balzac associated with the Anglo-Saxons :

> *Quoi qu'elle fasse ou dise, l'Angleterre est matérialiste.* . . . .
> *Elle possède au plus haut degré cette science de l'existence
> qui bonifie les moindres parcelles de la matérialité, qui fait
> que votre pantoufle est la plus exquise pantoufle du monde, qui
> donne à votre linge une saveur indicible, qui double de cèdre
> et parfume les commodes; qui verse à l'heure dite un thé
> suave . . . qui bannit la poussière . . . brosse les murs des caves,
> polit le marteau de la porte, assouplit les ressorts du carrosse,
> qui fait de la matière une poulpe nourrissante et cotonneuse,
> brilliante et propre, au sein de laquelle l'âme expire sous la
> jouissance . . . Ainsi je connus tout à coup . . . une femme,
> peut-être unique en son sexe, qui m'enveloppa dans les rets
> de cet amour renaissant de son agonie, et aux prodigalités
> duquel j'apportais une continence sévère. . . . La nuit, je
> pleurais de bonheur; la matin, je pleurais de remords . . .*

Yet, though Lady Dudley may be phantasmagoric, she
has a poetic truth. And here, I think, we begin to approach
the secret of Balzac's creative genius—his faculty of assimilat-
ing the real and temporal without permitting himself for a
moment to become its slave. No writer has ever been more
unashamed, more superbly unselfconscious. We have only
to compare Balzac and Flaubert (a martyr of his own sensitiveness and literary good taste) to feel again the superiority
of Balzac's gift. Balzac's taste was variable or non-existent.
His psychology was erratic (though almost invariably
sound). He was occasionally vulgar; but his vulgarity was
pitched in the heroic key. Put side by side with the masterpieces of the modern novelist, who tempers alarming
realism with disarming sentimentality, who purveys intel-
lectualism in a predigested form or who attempts to
suffocate the critical faculty beneath a weight of words,

Balzac's achievement is the more astonishing. He could write very long books which seem as brief as *Les Illusions Perdues*, or short books which seem as full and packed with meaning as *Le Lys dans la Vallée*. All bear the stamp of that poetic veracity which discards naturalism for the " super-realism " of the greatest literature.

HONORÉ BALZAC

George Borrow

THAT FEW human beings are qualified to tell the truth is an observation frequently forced upon us by our reading of history and biography; and there is much, therefore, to recommend an autobiographical work the author of which makes no effort to tell the " whole truth," in the teeth of the difficulties raised by his education and temperament, but allows feelings rather than facts to form the basis of his narrative. After all, in the individual life, it is our emotional response to an event, not the event itself, that is usually of real and lasting consequence: and the evasions and agonised deceptions of a Jean—Jacques Rousseau are at least as significant as his approximations to historical accuracy. Every literature can show us one or more of those books in which the " real " and the " imaginary " are permitted to intermingle and the truth that emerges is primarily subjective. Such is the exquisite *Florentine Nights* of Heine: such, in our own language, George Borrow's record of his youth and adolescence. For many readers, that fascinating book is doomed by a single scrap of hackneyed dialogue: but in its proper context Jasper Petulengro's reference to the wind upon the heath loses its air of having been specially composed for a Christmas gift-calendar or cheap-jack prose anthology. Borrow was anything but a professor of specious literary optimism. Vague melancholy enshrouded him from youth to age—now evanescent, scarcely perceptible like a delicate autumn mist which adds softness and poetic depth to an October landscape: now thickening and darkening, till he was in the grip of the nightmare state that he called " the horrors," and raved and trembled and was obsessed by the idea of suicide.

In his preface to the first edition, Borrow describes *Lavengro* as " a dream partly of study, partly of adventure." A dream it is—like a drawing by Dadd or an etching by Piranesi; and through its dream perspectives strays the apparition of its curious author, brown-faced, solemn-eyed, prematurely silver-haired, a kind of White Knight, burdened with a fantastic load of very often entirely useless erudition: the vocabularies of remote languages he had never completely mastered: translations no English publisher would agree to undertake: fragments of Basque and a rag-bag hoard of Romany idiom, with a toppling pile of Bibles to crown the load—all cobbled together with a queer network of beliefs and prejudices. Both as a translator and a recorder of fact, Borrow proves at the best of times to have been remarkably inaccurate. But he was no mendacious windbag of the Trelawny stamp; for, while Trelawny's mind was in some respects as coarse and commonplace as his nature was violent, unscrupulous and untrustworthy, through Borrow's composition ran a profoundly poetic strain. He was dominated by a sense of the mystery of life: Trelawny by a feeling for its superficial melodrama. The Younger Son lies flatly, blatantly, boldly: Lavengro does not falsify so much as transform his recollections, encouraging his memory to play the alchemist and extract the quintessence of the material it had hoarded up, sharpening the outlines of remembered experience, strengthening its colours. What did he himself see, and what imagine? Again and again, he appears to make no very definite distinction between what he had, and what he *might* have, done and witnessed. Certainly (as his biographer, Professor Knapp, has established with an infinity of trouble) he did not see and take off his hat to the great trotting stallion, Marshland Shales, in the hurlyburly of a Norwich ¡horse-fair ' in 1818; for Marshland Shales was not paraded there till 1827. Equally ill-established—at least as regards chronology and minor details—are many other striking and dramatic episodes. But, if they did not happen in time and space—at Norwich or Edinburgh or among the bogs of Ireland—they occurred without a doubt in Borrow's imagination; and in those surroundings, and in that climate, they have their own validity.

Naturally, George Borrow is Borrow's hero. He is an unusual hero, however—not always brave, far from resolute, in no career that he undertakes conspicuously successful, a moody, gloomy, pottering, reflective personage. All he asks is that we should regard him as a highly exceptional being, in the sense that, for good or ill, he is not as other men. Portents have attended him from early childhood. He has a strange power over poisonous snakes, a way with horses. In the nursery he is at first uncommonly dull and silent—but the Jewish pedlar notes at once that he is a gifted child—afterwards an extremely voracious reader. Instead of acquiring Greek, he learns Irish: when he is articled to the law, he engages in an intensive study of a mediæval Welsh poet, the celebrated Ab Gwilym. Yet his studies (he is prepared to admit) are fragmentary and undisciplined: for the point he emphasises is not his genius but his personal separateness—the isolation that is the constant background of his thoughts and feelings. Lavengro is a lonely man with a thousand casual acquaintances—a man whose life is full of incidents and interests, but has little continuity. He drifts at large through the world, which flows cloudily past him. It is the panorama of a dream—inconsequent as are many dreams, but endowed with a visionary magnitude and a dream-like vividness.

Borrow's sense of his own identity—and his self-portrait of a certain type of lonely, ineffective, thoughtful man—holds the narrative together from opening to closing chapters. We have all of us known such self-centred solitaries: but, whereas that type of egotism is usually dim and arid, Borrow turned his self-absorption to brilliant creative profit. Not many other modern writers have been able to give so pungent an air of individuality to the scenes or the personages that they describe: none can make more of a single unrelated incident. Borrow's finest passages are unforgettable: the impression they leave on the reader's imagination is never quite effaced. From a stubble-field rises the tall shape of the ancient viper-hunter, with his gaiters and skin-cap and his bag of struggling reptiles: on a cliff-edge squats red-coated David Haggart, drummer-boy and future felon, gazing out over the smoky confusion of Edinburgh house-tops: or through a snow-storm comes leaping the Irish warlock, snowflakes crusted on his shoulders, a raw, terrible wound cutting his forehead and, bounding at his heels, the ferocious " dog of peace."

Thanks to the researches of Borrow's editors and biographers, it is now possible to identify many of his subjects, whose names in the original text of *Lavengro* are omitted or represented by a dash. A number of them were natives of East Anglia, where Borrow's father, after long regimental wanderings, ultimately settled down. There is Joseph John Gurney, the Quaker banker and philanthropist, brother to Mrs. Fry: William Taylor, an enthusiast for German literature and the correspondent of Godwin, Scott and Southey, who infected the young Borrow with infidel notions: John Thurtell—a particularly incisive portrait—

in whose appearance " there was a blending of the bluff and
the sharp," sternness " with something approaching to the
feline," destined to be hanged at Hereford for the murder
of a fellow swindler: and later, when Borrow removes to
London, that terrifying Grub Street tyrant, Sir Richard
Phillips, hosier, stationer, publisher, Radical vegetarian,
who set the writer to compiling *Newgate Lives and Trials*,
from which he imbibed " strange doubts " about crime and
virtue, till the necessitarian notions of his boyhood again
obscured his fancy, and " my own peculiar ideas with
respect to everything being a lying dream began also to
revive."

" I had (confesses Borrow) a very ill-regulated mind at
that period." But it is difficult to think of any period at
which the nature of his beliefs and the play of his speculation
were not strikingly eccentric. That unregulated, undisciplined quality is part of his book's charm. *Lavengro* was
written between 1843 and 1850: the scenes and personages
he describes belong mostly to the epoch of the Napoleonic
Wars: and, thanks both to the distance from his material
at which he was composing, and to the faculty of enlargement his eye possessed, the landscapes he evokes are
generally larger than life-size. Berwick-upon-Tweed, above
its broad green river from which robust fishermen are
drawing huge silver-mailed salmon, becomes " a white old
city, surrounded with lofty walls . . ." London Bridge
undergoes a mystical metamorphosis:

A strange kind of bridge it was; huge and massive,
and seemingly of great antiquity. It had an arched back,
like that of a hog, a high balustrade, and at either side,
at intervals, were stone bowers bulking over the river. . . .
Though the bridge was wide—very wide—it was all too
narrow for the concourse upon it. Thousands of human

beings were pouring over the bridge. But what chiefly struck my attention was the double row of carts and wagons, the generality drawn by horses as large as elephants, each row striving hard in a different direction, and not infrequently brought to a standstill. Oh, the cracking of whips, the shouts and oaths of the carters, and the grating of wheels upon the enormous stones that formed the pavements! . . . But, if upon the bridge there was a confusion, below it there was a confusion ten times confounded. The tide, which was fast ebbing, obstructed by the immense piers of the old bridge, poured beneath the arches with a fall of several feet, forming in the river below as many whirlpools as there were arches. Truly tremendous was the roar of the descending waters, and the bellow of the tremendous gulfs, which swallowed them for a time, and then cast them forth. . . . Slowly advancing along the bridge, I came to the highest point, and there I stood still . . . just above the principal arch, looking through the balustrade at the scene that presented itself—and such a scene!

It was here, of course, in one of these stone-balustraded recesses, high over the whirlpools of the tumultuous river, that, for the second time during his life, Borrow encountered Defoe and succumbed to the fascination of the earliest and, in some respects, the greatest of English realistic novels. Nothing in Borrow's existence could happen simply. *Robinson Crusoe* had irradiated and transformed his childhood: *Moll Flanders*, which also reached him by a stroke of fortune, imparted new significance to his London life:

I took the book from her hand; a short, thick volume, at least a century old, bound with greasy black leather. I turned the yellow and dog's-eared pages, reading here and there a sentence. Yes, and no mistake! *His* pen, his style, his spirit might be observed in every line . . . I covered my face with my hand, and thought of my childhood. . . .

" This is a singular book," said I at last. . . .

The extent of Borrow's indebtedness to Defoe is sufficiently clear: but equally obvious are the differences in their approach and outlook. Defoe's most impressive passages are built up of a painstaking accumulation of prosaic details—it is through the addition of one fact to another that, little by little, he achieves effects of surprising dignity: Borrow's grasp of an historical fact is subordinate to his appreciation of its emotional context. Borrow could not have completed a *Moll Flanders*: but then, Defoe could not have written the story of the man who believed in the magic touch or of the Welsh preacher who had committed the sin against the Holy Ghost—two absorbing studies of psychological malady. Borrow belonged to a revolutionary experimental age which, though it left the world an uglier, harsher, more confusing place, immensely enlarged the frontiers of the human consciousness. The limitations of the nineteenth-century mind, and the spiritual *malaise* and flashes of poetic insight by which it was often visited, receive illustration in the diversity and complexity of Borrow's dream-novel.

'Our Mutual Friend'

IT WOULD be interesting to know how many adult English readers have recently re-read a novel by Dickens, how thoroughly and with what measure of appreciation. For the average Englishman, Dickens belongs to adolescence. During later life, he is prepared, theoretically at least, to concede the novelist all manner of literary virtues; but, if pressed, he would be hard put to it to define those qualities. The associations of childhood are omnipresent. In fact, though Dickens has a variety of characteristics that recommend him to the young, his chief qualities—and, incidentally, his greatest vices—are appreciable only by an adult critical sense. The purveyor of blameless fiction, and wholesale manufacturer of narratives that have found their way unquestioned into every school library, was among the most complex and curious artists that have yet appeared—a writer in whom every apparent simplicity proves on closer inspection to conceal an ambiguity and who composed, so to speak, both with the right and with the left hand, one member seldom entirely conscious of what the other did. To appreciate his strangeness to the full, it is instructive to begin with a novel that is either completely unfamiliar or of which the impression has been almost obliterated during the course of time. *Our Mutual Friend* may provide a convenient starting-point. Less hackneyed than *Bleak House* or *David*

152

Copperfield, it contains passages as splendid as anything
that is to be found in either novel. It displays the writer's
genius at its very highest concentration, but also exhibits
his astounding drawbacks.

A journey through *Our Mutual Friend* is prolific of
surprises and, during its latter stages, attended by many
crushing disappointments. Few stories begin so well. It
is with a feeling of exhilaration—almost with the excitement
of some brilliant new discovery—that we release ourselves
on the rushing stream of the author's narrative, swing round
on the swift current of his verbal fantasy, are swept in and
out of the extraordinary backwaters of his imagination.
What a prodigious love of, and what an unfailing skill in,
the use of words and images! The juxtaposition of the first
and second episodes—Jesse Hexam and his daughter fishing
for corpses among the Thames-side wharves, the Veneerings
and their hangers-on busy with a more conventional kind
of scavenging—is a bold device and, by the effect it produces,
completely justified. Already a vision of London is develop-
ing in the reader's mind: the vast mysterious gloomy river
and the tight-packed congeries of ancient wooden buildings,
taverns, warehouses, stairs and jetties that scramble down
its banks: grim squares, with crossing-sweepers and
gingerbread-sellers huddled near black Georgian railings,
and pale footmen yawning in foggy entrance halls: coaches
and chariots in the mud, and helpless drunkards asleep amid
the cabbage leaves and horse-droppings of Covent Garden.

From every damp crevice emerges some fresh remarkable
personage; and the novelist's genius envelops and absorbs
them all. Dinner at the Veneerings' is a magnificent *tour de
force*. Like the creations of myth, these diners-out are both
terrible and comic. That Dickens in certain aspects has an
unexpected affinity to Marcel Proust—that his verbal con-
structions now and then are nearly as complicated, very

often as subtle and as fantastic—was pointed out not long ago by an ingenious Englishess ayist. But there is an additional resemblance in the enthusiastic detachment with which he depicts many of his characters—those with whom the sympathies of his heart did not, at the very outset, become unfortunately, and sometimes fatally, involved. Albertine is an example of Proust's failure to compose a portrait, when his own feelings and secret prejudices rose in a misty veil between artist and subject. The characters that Dickens failed to realise are too exasperating and too notorious to deserve enumeration. But each novelist was a master of the minor personage, examined under the bright lens of an incomparable poetic gift which glorified as it enlarged, and illumined the essential oddity of every object on which it rested.

This process of magnification or mythological enlargement is seen at its best in the account of the Veneerings' dinner-party. Dickens's literary impressionism is much in evidence. His affinity with Proust need not be laboured: just as striking are the suggestions of Henry James, Joyce and several other modern English novelists:

The great looking-glass above the sideboard reflects the table and the company. Reflects the new Veneering crest, in gold and eke in silver, frosted and also thawed, a camel of all work. . . . Reflects Veneering; forty, wavy-haired, dark, tending to corpulence, sly, mysterious, filmy —a kind of sufficiently well-looking veiled prophet, not prophesying. Reflects Mrs. Veneering; fair, aquiline-nosed and fingered, not so much light hair as she might have, gorgeous in raiment and jewels, enthusiastic, propitiatory, conscious that a corner of her husband's veil is over herself. Reflects Podsnap; prosperously feeding. . . . Reflects Mrs. Podsnap; fine woman for Professor

Owen, quantity of bone, neck and nostrils like a rocking-horse, hard features, majestic headdress in which Podsnap has hung golden offerings. Reflects Twemlow; grey, dry, polite, susceptible to east wind. . . . Reflects mature young lady; raven locks, and complexion that lights up well when well powdered—as it is—carrying on considerably in the captivation of mature young gentleman; with too much nose in his face, too much ginger in his whiskers, too much torso in his waistcoat, too much sparkle in his studs, his eyes, his buttons, his talk, and his teeth. Reflects charming old Lady Tippins on Veneering's right; with an immense obtuse drab oblong face, like a face in a tablespoon, and a dyed Long Walk up the top of her head, as a convenient public approach to the bunch of false hair behind, pleased to patronise Mrs. Veneering opposite who is pleased to be patronised.

Here Dickens's humour is as hard and unkind as the light of the dinner-table. The Veneerings are " bran-new people," City people, diligent social climbers. Every acquaintance whom they can attract becomes, automatically and instantaneously, an " oldest friend." Poor little Mr. Twemlow (own cousin to an earl and a professional diner-out, though he lodges over a livery stable yard in Duke Street, St. James's) spends hours with nervous hand pressed to his tight aching forehead, as he meditates the insoluble problem of the Veneerings' social alchemy—how so many " oldest friends " can be conjured up at such short notice out of nothing; while the Veneerings' butler (known as the Analytical Chemist from the cautious and disbelieving manner in which he handles dishes and decanters) adds a touch of macabre scepticism to the background of his employers' triumphs.

It was a particularly happy thought, from the stream of

casual chit-chat round the Veneerings' table, to produce the main theme (or what purports to be the main theme) of *Our Mutual Friend*—the search for the heir to old Harmon's dust-raised fortune. The dust-landscape round Boffin's Bower comes mysteriously to life in Mortimer's languid gossip:

> " The man," Mortimer goes on, addressing Eugene, " whose name is Harmon, was the only son of a tremendous old rascal who made his money by Dust."
>
> " Red velveteens and a bell? " the gloomy Eugene enquires.
>
> " And a ladder and basket if you like. By which means, or others, he grew rich as a Dust Contractor, and lived in a hollow in a hilly country entirely composed of Dust. On his own small estate the growling old vagabond threw up his own mountain range, like an old volcano, and its geological formation was Dust. Coal-dust, vegetable-dust, bone-dust, crockery dust, rough dust, and sifted dust—all manner of Dust."

Among surroundings as odd as these, and on the same level of sinister imagination, the story remains throughout the whole of Book the First. London itself is the chief character of these earlier episodes; other personages are real and significant in so far as they form a part of the London scene. It is London that fills them out—gives them colour and energy. The characters who impress us most are the men and women whose urban habitat is best established: the Veneerings in their vast, new, vulgar, over-varnished house; the Podsnaps, occupants of " a shady angle adjoining Portman Square," full of massive furniture, heavy plate, walnut and rosewood tables and " swarthy giants of looking-glasses "; Mr. Wilfer going home to his cottage in Holloway across " a tract of suburban Sahara, where tiles and bricks were burnt, bones were boiled, carpets were beat, rubbish was shot, dogs were fought " and numerous kiln-fires made lurid smudges on the encircling fog-wall; Mr. Venus, in his little shop in the Clerkenwell back street (with the two preserved frogs in the windows fighting an endless duel), among the disarticulated odds and ends of half a dozen human skeletons.

Up to this point the reader's progress is rapid and adventurous. Then, gradually, a change occurs; for all the acuteness of their outline, he becomes aware that there is something surprisingly two-dimensional about Dickens's characters; and the Dolls' Dressmaker pops into dreadful prominence at the opening of Book the Second. Most odious of the author's creations, Miss Jenny Wren, would be less insufferable did a horrid vitality not inform her portrait. Miss Wren incorporates one of Dickens's favourite obsessions—the reversal of the ordinary child-parent situation. Both she and Bella Wilfer " mother " their fathers—Bella tenderly, almost amorously, with teasing and hair-pulling: Jenny, thriving on disappointment, with ogreish zest. The novelist himself is far too stirred to be quite dispassionate. For Dickens the contemplation of virtue—particularly feminine virtue—would appear often to have been a means of sensuous self-indulgence; and the more he revels in the idea of virtue, the weaker and vaguer seems his grasp of any idea of goodness.

Thus *Our Mutual Friend* is a crowded, but an extremely empty, book. It has an enormous ramifying plot; but that plot, if attentively examined, proves to be full of false starts, dead ends and clues that lead nowhere. An important aspect of the original design is a study of the effect of wealth on human character. From being a harmless eccentric, Mr. Boffin becomes a tyrannous and grasping crank. Yet, in the last section, his creator—overwhelmed, apparently by a rush of universal optimism—decides to cover Boffin's sins with a coat of whitewash, but slaps it on with such an exhausted, or such a reckless, hand as to involve himself in several major inconsistencies and completely destroy the real sense of his previous portrait. This mistake might itself have been unimportant, were it not symptomatic of a flaw that runs through the whole conception—the absence, amid brilliant stylistic virtues, of a genuine sense of style. One of the tragedies of nineteenth-century English literature was that it should produce so many colossi in clay from the knees down, that it should have made genius almost synonymous with incompleteness. *Our Mutual Friend* is nearly a masterpiece—not quite an appalling failure. But both its qualities and its shortcomings are on the scale of an heroic age.

Rudyard Kipling

To-DAY, WHEN almost every subject of first-rate biographical interest has been handled and re-handled, used and mis-used, the prospective biographer can still fall back upon a comforting reflection: we know little more of the nature of the creative gift—of its origins and development, of its connection with a writer's social circumstances on the one hand, his physical constitution on the other—than did Johnson when he wrote the *Lives of the Poets* or Boswell when he introduced the modern art of biography by com-piling the *Life of Johnson*. The mechanism of the creative impulse remains largely unexplored. We have grasped the fact that the experiences of early youth—for example Baudelaire's jealous love of his mother and hatred of his step-father—may give a specially acute twist to the direction of a writer's talent: that physical flaws—Sterne's consumptive tendency, or the disease of the inner ear that distracted Jonathan Swift—may exert a profound influence on the artist's character and outlook. But we cannot decide why the same factors, that cause breakdown and disintegration in ninety-nine out of a hundred perplexed and tormented human beings, in the hundredth or the thousandth become a source of spiritual strength and creative energy: why some minds have a knack of maintaining their conflicts in a state

159

of fruitful equilibrium: why an artist may fail in life to succeed on the plane of art.

Beside this central problem, any fresh discoveries a biographer may make have a merely relative importance; and there is an obvious danger that the critic who casts some new sidelight upon an artist's psychological background will give the impression that he thinks he has *explained* him. Such an impression—perhaps inadvertently—has been conveyed both by Mr. Edmund Wilson, in his essay on Rudyard Kipling, published among other penetrating essays in *The Wound and the Bow*, and by Kipling's latest biographer, Mr. Hilton Brown.[1] Each helps to elucidate Kipling, assembles and arranges some illuminating scraps of information: neither can explain why his peculiar personal genius took the course it did. Each study, nevertheless, contains some brilliant guesswork. They agree, for instance, that a miserable childhood, when Kipling and his sister were abandoned by their parents to the care of sadistic guardians, followed by the brutalities of an English public school, left scars on the writer's spirit which stayed with him all his life; and that the experience of having been very much bullied and, for several impressionable years, being very much afraid, may have determined Kipling's attitude to the forces of law and order. He emerged from jungle life with a respect for the law of the jungle. Himself weak and physically dependent, he had learned to despise those " lesser breeds without the law " who constitute, under an imperialist system, nature's subject-races. There was a moment, says Edmund Wilson, when his outlook was more liberal, and the range of his social sympathies was far more generous. Did he not prophesy the evolution of a many-rooted American race?

[1] *Rudyard Kipling: A New Appreciation.* By Hilton Brown. Hamish Hamilton.

Wait till the Anglo-American-German-Jew-the-Man-of-the-Future—is properly equipped. . . . He'll carry the English lungs above the Teuton feet that can walk for-ever; and he will wave long, thin, bony Yankee hands with the big blue veins on the wrist, from one end of the earth to the other. He'll be the finest writer, poet and dramatist . . . that the world as it recollects itself has ever seen. By virtue of his Jew blood—just a little, little drop —he'll be a musician and a painter, too.

But, alas, Kipling's residence in America (which lasted from 1892 to 1896) was cut short by an undignified quarrel with his troublesome and truculent American brother-in-law. His daughter, Josephine, whom he appears to have loved more deeply and devotedly than he loved any other human being, died in New York on his brief return to America during the year 1899; and Kipling fled for refuge to the solid amenities of conservative English life. According to Wilson's view, he " invoked the protection of the British system and at the same time prostrated himself before the power of British conquest. . . . " He became the prophet of imperialist expansion, at a juncture when the imperial dream had reached its headiest stages.

So far the historian elucidates; and at this point it is not difficult for the critic, particularly if he belongs to the Left Wing, to absolve himself from further effort by relapsing into a condition of voluntary amnesia. He need only re-capitulate some of Kipling's better-known and more unpleasing phrases—to remind himself of the admiration of brute force that appears in many stories, to recall *The Mark of the Beast* with its sadistic imagery, or the " dose of cleaning-rod " which Tommy Atkins boasts of having handed out to various recalcitrant and unappreciative " niggers." Kipling would be easy to damn, were a writer's value in direct proportion to that of his social and political philosophy. As " thinkers " or political soothsayers, artists, even the finest, are often conspicuously misguided. Kipling was an extraordinarily accomplished artist; and what is significant is not the worth of his opinions themselves so much as the artistic use to which he put them, and the intellectual limitations that he revealed by adopting them so uncritically and so wholeheartedly. May we not infer, suggests Mr. Hilton Brown, that he was " fundamentally uninterested in political questions "? Yet " he felt it incumbent on him to strike an attitude and in this, once assumed, he petrified. The result was that between his first-class intellect and his second-hand political opinions there was a constant and unresolved conflict which, if it was never obvious to himself, was always fatally obvious to his enemies." Faced with the question why he felt obliged to strike an attitude, instead of allowing himself to develop along those lines of direct observation and graphic description for which he was so admirably suited, his new biographer replies that the habit of proselytism was in Kipling's blood:

We see a preacher—one might almost say, a prophet—by birth and inclination; the hardheaded, proselytising North County Methodist, confused but inspired by the mystic and superstitious Celt. He has a mission to instruct. . . . His early upbringing is stormy, at times penitential; it instils in him a need for privacy and independence and a distrust in man which may become under suitable stimuli . . . the germ of a distrust in God.

Here we return from the worth or worthlessness of Kipling's ideas to the peculiar characteristics of the mind by which they were received and fostered. Mr. Hilton Brown speaks of "petrification"; but the word was unhappily chosen. If Kipling failed to become the great modern novelist, the " English Balzac " whom Henry James had foreseen and welcomed, if most of his stories are deformed, here and there, by inexplicable faults of taste and exasperating tricks of style—for instance, the sham Biblical idiom he always much affected—it was not because he had " wrong " ideas or had suffered disabling experiences during childhood and maturity—the ideas were a symptom: the experiences he underwent might well have been surmounted —but because his genius, in the last resort, was curiously immature. He had known India as a very young man: his famous Indian stories have the clarity of a young man's vision, accompanied by its drawbacks. He simplified his view of life with the help of a schoolboy's code. He retained a schoolboy's love of mystification—again and again he hints at secrets that cannot be divulged, knowledge he cannot communicate: " that " (he is fond of repeating) " is another story "—together with a schoolboy's passion for machinery, for the things that work, for a trim mechanical universe that does not admit the bewildering complexity of adult human feelings.

Thus the consummate artist—for no one who studies words, or, on his own account, has ever attempted to write a story, can deny that Kipling was an artist of superb accomplishment—failed to conquer the heights of self-expression that appeared to be his birthright. He paused at a certain distance, like Moses contemplating the blue perspectives of a far-off Promised Land—one of those incomplete men of genius, so numerous in the astonishing literature of the English-speaking races. Yet, as a creative intelligence at least, Kipling did not petrify. It is an odd fact—one that comes home to us with a shock of surprise when we are considering his progress—that the darker, more troubled side of his mind grew more and more pronounced as he travelled towards old age. Just as *The Brushwood Boy* has two facets, which mirror alternately the real and the dream world, a real world of duties and conventions, a dreamland of nameless fears and irresponsible imaginings, so Kipling's spirit had a light and a dark side, a harshly dogmatic and a dreamily pessimistic, or romantically defeatist, strain. *Debits and Credits*, published in 1926, and *Limits and Renewals*, published in 1932, contain stories that, had they been the work of a young and unknown writer, the average editor might have condemned as ridiculously obscure or dismissed as perversely morbid. Some, like *Dayspring Mishandled* and *Unprofessional*, show a Jamesian indirectness of approach and involution of technique, unrelieved, however, by Henry James's extraordinary powers of penetration; and a reader struggles through to the closing paragraph with only the very vaguest conception of the story's theme and purport. Even more striking is the regular reappearance of certain types of subject. *Dayspring Mishandled* unfolds a gloomy labyrinth of treachery, disease and death. *The Woman in His Life*, a sentimental dog-story, starts off with a vivid description of a harrowing nervous breakdown. *Unprofessional* is based on cancer and suicide. *The Wish House*, one of Kipling's most horrible fantasies, reverts to the subject of cancer, which, in this instance, is represented as a direct result of witchcraft. *A Madonna of the Trenches* is a study of suicide, in a setting of shell-shocked hysteria and ghostly visitation. *The Gardener*, which deserves to rank high in the Kipling canon, deals with a mysterious mourner and an unacknowledged love. That last effort is particularly effective and highly typical. It has the customary faults of taste—here the apparition of Christ as a gardener of war-graves; it also reveals Kipling's talents in the purely dramatic order. Helen meets Mrs. Scarsworth, who tells her that she has been commissioned to photograph graves, at a dismal Belgian inn:

Mrs. Scarsworth had backed against the shut door, and her mouth worked dryly.

. . ." You—you know about those graves of mine I was telling you about downstairs, just now? They really *are* commissions. At least, several of them are." Her eyes wandered round the room. " What extraordinary wall-papers they have in Belgium, don't you think? . . . Yes, I swear they are commissions. But there's *one*, d'you see, and—and he was more to me than anything else in the world. Do you understand? . . . Of course, he oughtn't to have been. He ought to have been nothing to me. But he *was*. He *is*. That's why I do the commissions, you see. That's all."

" But why do you tell me? " Helen asked desperately.

" Because I'm *so* tired of lying. . . . He was everything to me that he oughtn't to have been—the one real thing —the only thing that ever happened to me in all my life; and I've had to pretend he wasn't. . . . I've gone to him eight times. . . . To-morrow'll make the ninth, and—and I can't—I *can't* go to him again with nobody in the world knowing. I want to be honest with some one before I go. Do you understand? It doesn't matter about *me*. I was never truthful even as a girl. . . ."

She lifted her joined hands almost to the level of her mouth, and brought them down sharply, still joined, to full arms' length below her waist. Helen reached forward, caught them, bowed her head over them, and murmured: " Oh, my dear! My dear! " Mrs. Scarsworth stepped back, her face all mottled.

" My God! " she said. " Is *that* how you take it."

No, Kipling's talents did not decay. They remained in

suspense, just as the conflicts behind them remained permanently unresolved—or, perhaps it would be more accurate to say, permanently unassimilated. The waking man and the dreamer—the prophet and the artist—were still at variance when he published his tantalising autobiography, that masterpiece of suppression and understatement, in 1937.

H. G. Wells

In mid-August 1946 died H. G. Wells, " peacefully," at his London house, one of a majestic terrace overlooking Regent's Park. Little had been heard of him during the last few months; but old friends who occasionally crossed his threshold spoke of the veteran world-planner as growing tired and fretful—" tired as a sick child " was Desmond McCarthy's phrase—oppressed by the realisation of all his worst forebodings and dejected by the apparent bankruptcy of the innumerable hopes and schemes that he had sprung from his own spiritual viscera for more than half a century. Now his optimism had reached its limits; and the twilight of the prophet's existence was gloomy and unrelieved. His contribution had long ago been made; nothing he had recently added seemed likely to increase its value; but the obituary notices, when they appeared—tributes which ranged from the dignified insipidity of a *Times* editorial to a paragraph of measured depreciation published in the *Tablet*—agreed that in H. G. Wells we had lost one of the most representative literary figures to emerge since 1890.

Otherwise, whether friendly or hostile, the writers of these notices were not very successful in their attempts to supply a balanced portrait. They spoke of the diversity of his achievement and of the continuity of his purpose; of the vigour of his mind and of his obvious limitations. They

167

wrote with warm appreciation of the early novels and of the scientific fantasies; they could not explain the transition from books they admired to books they found less admirable, or the gradual diffusion of his literary gifts that characterised the later periods of his gigantic lifework. The task was evidently beyond them. Indeed, one would require Wells's own knack of compression, and perhaps something more than Wells's imaginative insight, to chart the astonishing course on which his mind had travelled, or to summarise the temperamental gear and the intellectual bag-and-baggage the traveller carried with him. Himself he was often impatient of the past, and intolerant of the burdens that tradition lays upon us. Yet, it is impossible to understand Wells unless we understand his background; and his background was complex and curious, being made up of two contrasted but inter-related pictures, drawn from different aspects of modern English history.

On the one hand, we see a mean shop and a perspective of shabby streets; on the other, an English country house, independent, aloof, tranquil, still girt around with all the apparatus of semi-feudal splendour. Uppark had romantic links with the life of an earlier century; for Sir Henry Fetherstonhaugh, who inherited the house and estate as a gay and rakish young man in 1774, kept among his early mistresses a girl called Emma Hart (afterwards notorious as Nelson's Lady Hamilton), and cut an extravagant dash at the court of George IV. In his old age, he married and settled down, his choice falling on a country girl—by some accounts a dairymaid—whom he had previously had educated in all the proper social elegances; and the sister of this Lady Fetherstonhaugh was still living at Uppark, among Sir Henry's fine eighteenth-century furniture, in the year 1880, when Sarah Wells, the wife of an unsuccessful and improvident tradesman, was promoted to the rank of housekeeper, to rule over footmen and maid servants in satin and lace cap. The scale of life at Uppark was generous and patriarchal. Mrs. Wells's children often visited her, spending months at a time about the house and gardens. The most promising was " Bert," a fragile, sandy-haired little boy with a long inquiring upper lip. He rummaged among Sir Henry's books and examined the stars through an old telescope that he had found and reassembled.

There can be no doubt of the decisive influence of these childish " below-stairs " associations on H. G. Wells's development. It was not an influence that he himself denied, and in his *Experiment in Autobiography* he went so far as to acknowledge the debt that English civilisation owed to the life of its country houses, whose owners had been a bulwark of taste and a focus of liberal thought. One is bound to add, nevertheless, that behind any gratitude he may have felt was a tinge of mistrust and an undercurrent of resentment. It is interesting, for example, that, although Uppark is one of the most beautiful houses of its kind that still exist in England, the beauty of his surroundings should have left him totally unimpressed, and that he should have dismissed them in his autobiography with a brief and chilly phrase, observing that the mansion was " a handsome great house looking southward, with beach woods and bracken thickets to shelter the dappled fallow deer of its wide undulating downland park." In *Tono Bungay*, which deals at length with this phase of his evolution, he is scarcely more expansive; and it is hard to resist the conclusion that life in the great house—and its associations, if not with the sense of servitude, at least with the idea of social inferiority and economic helplessness—bred in him a psychological opposition to certain forms of beauty, that it hardened and exaggerated the strain of philistinism which is always to be detected running through his life-work. He loved beauty when it was alive and sensuous: he feared and distrusted the beauty that is static, the grace that tradition has crystallised, on which time has laid a hand.

For always, looming large over his imagination, was the other aspect of his boyhood. Bromley, where his mother and father had brought up their children and, as incompetent shopkeepers, had struggled, floundered, worried, was already, at the end of the nineteenth century, being engulfed by London suburban squalor. Fields and woods were "developed"; streams were piped underground or dwindled to rusty rivulets; private enterprise flung out to right and left long, monotonous, yellowish streets of badly-built, inconvenient, unattractive houses. It struck Wells, early in his career as a thoughtful human being, that development of this kind was both essentially uneconomic and utterly unscrupulous, and that there was a connection between these manifestations of modern commercial enterprise and the conditions of his parents' life, their pathetic struggle and their endless, hopeless preoccupation with halfpennies, sixpences and shillings. Beneath the shop at Bromley was an underground kitchen, also used as a living-room; and there the family ate its meals, by the dim light that filtered from above through a grating in the pavement. He looked up at the pavement-grating and watched the boot-soles of passers-by as they hurried down Bromley High Street. From his privileged position, he was able to observe that they were generally worn through.

Back to Uppark Park again, where the dappled fallow deer grazed on the turf, and Sarah Wells, in the white-panelled housekeeper's room, a small defeated figure, rigidly respectable and timidly inefficient, took refuge from harsh reality in a world of pious platitudes. What was the connection between Uppark and Bromley? The great house continued to stand firm, but the social system that it symbolised was rapidly decaying. Round these oases of calm and dignity, a new universe of squalor and confusion was being fast created, a universe dominated not by aristocrats of the traditional stamp—the men who had built Uppark and stocked its library shelves—but by adventurers of a strange and alarming type, possessed of titanic energy but entirely innocent either of an inherited sense of social responsibility or of the revolutionary ability to look and plan ahead. They were changing England, and they were changing Europe. The consequences of the change, the implications of the upheaval they had created, were subjects that did not concern them: the future might take care of itself.

Here one must make an exceedingly important point. A conviction of social injustice, in the narrowest, most abstract sense, cannot be included among Wells's ruling motives. His aspirations were completely practical. First came a passionate desire for personal emancipation, a longing to escape himself from the deadening pressure of his economic circumstances. He escaped with the help of education, and the education he acquired was primarily scientific. Had it been classical or historical, the evolution of his mind might have proceeded very differently, and what he lost in impetus he might have gained in breadth of vision. But the message of science, at the time when Wells absorbed it from the lectures of J. H. Huxley, was still positive and cocksure. In those days, there were no mystical physicists, no philosophical astronomers, to confound us with a hint that science itself had definite limitations. Science supplied the assurance that the young man was in search of; and from science he graduated to Socialism and, having lost patience with Socialism of the cultivated Fabian school, Wells began to concoct a brand of Socialist teaching that would suit his own requirements. Confronted by the muddled landscape of late-Victorian England, where Uppark co-existed with Bromley, and blind tradition lived cheek by jowl with the blind, undirected forces of private commercial enterprise, he dreamed of the master-plan that was destined to replace them both, of a world reorganised by science through the agency of men who, like himself, had received the supreme benefit of a scientific training.

Yet Wells did not conform in his youth, nor would he ever conform, to the conventional pattern of the revolutionary Socialist. Lenin, when they met in the Kremlin, described him in conversation afterwards as a typical *petit bourgeois*; and Wells all his life remained persistently—even bitterly—critical of the orthodox Marxist creed. He deplored the worst excesses of individualism; but he was still an individualist, a practical thinker who, having solved his own economic problem, was now anxious to help in the clearing up of some of the preposterous muddles, private and public, he watched proliferating all around him. He was tidy in his mind and methods, whereas the methods of the militant revolutionary are lavish and extravagant. He abhorred waste; and no revolution can be made without a reckless expenditure of human lives and happiness. To that extent, he was *bourgeois*. He lacked, moreover, the cold mystical fire of the revolutionary agent; and it was not anger against society that inspired him year after year to prophesy, preach and proselytise, so much as the sheer impatience he felt at the sight of human inefficiency. The remedy was clear —so brilliantly clear—if the confused reader would have the goodness for a moment to borrow H. G. Wells's spectacles!

His impatience increased as time went on. And, as it increased, the rôle of the artist in his literary life grew more and more subsidiary. The artist, he suspected, must get in the planner's way. He would repudiate art. Yet it is an odd fact that his career, from one point of view, may be interpreted as a justification of aestheticism, since it demonstrates that for a writer to think aloud in print, however clearly and consistently, is seldom quite enough: that a whisper may be as influential as a loud emphatic statement: that there are more things in heaven and earth than were ever dreamed of at Huxley's feet in the classrooms of South Kensington. The situation would be simpler if Wells had been simply a bad artist, or a journalist to whom questions of art were totally irrelevant. On the contrary, he had uncommon artistic aptitude; the gift of selecting and placing words; an unusual faculty of description, and a fancy at once precise and sweeping; together with a sympathetic appreciation of his fellow human creatures.

No one who was not a magnificent story-teller could have carried to success the long and memorable series of scientific fantasies, in which his early technical training, at work on the imagination of a receptive literary artist, caused him to anticipate some of the most startling developments of the years 1914 to 1945. The scientific romances brought fame and security; and there followed a period when he experienced (he admitted himself) " a craving to figure as a novelist pure and simple," and wrote *Love and Mr. Lewisham, Kipps, Tono Bungay, Ann Veronica* and *The History of Mr. Polly.* There the artist was given his chance, but somehow failed to take it. At least, he failed to get the complete grasp of his material that makes a literary masterpiece; with the result that each of these books had many admirable passages, but none of them can be enjoyed as a finished æsthetic whole. They have vitality; but the life that animates them is diffuse and shapeless. Perhaps Wells despised perfection. It may be (as I have already suggested) that symmetry of form and beauty of detail were associated in his mind with the vision of Uppark, its graceful proportions, its harmonious setting. And what he denied himself, he tended to distrust in others.

Towards those contemporary writers most interested in literary form, Wells maintained an attitude of mocking incomprehension; and, while Henry James ventured in a friendly fashion to deplore Wells's tragic misuse of splendid natural faculties, Wells—equally friendly but somewhat more unguarded—made exuberant fun of Henry James in his agonised pursuit of the inevitable expressive word. For, if it is true that he came within measurable distance of being a great story-teller, it is also true that H. G. Wells was nearly a great satirist; and there are few happier essays in literary caricature than his imaginary account in *Boon* of a protracted conversation between Henry James and George Moore, the two accomplished stylists entirely at cross-purposes but each continuing to unfold his fine euphonious monologue; so that, while James is " labouring through the long cadences of his companion as an indefatigable steam-tug might labour endlessly against a rolling sea," piling parenthesis on parenthesis, and qualification on qualification, George Moore is engaged in describing, " with an extraordinary and loving mastery of detail . . . a glowing little experience that had been almost forced upon him at Nismes by a pretty little woman from Nebraska, and the peculiar effect it had had, and particularly the peculiar effect that the coincidence that both Nebraska and Nismes begin with an " N " and end so very differently, had had upon his imagination ": till they are suddenly interrupted by the uncouth apparition of the Editor of the *New Age*.

No account of Wells could pretend to completeness that did not include some reference to the youthful sense of fun, half affectionate, half malicious, which still thrust its way to the surface and threw up bubbling geysers, even in the products of his last decade, when his hopes for humanity as

H. G. *Wells*

a whole seemed to be steadily declining. Thus he had the
vehemence of a prophet but none of the solemnity. Ever and
again he would turn round on himself with an engagingly
candid smile, as who should say: " You are all muddlers—
incurable muddlers—but, at least when it comes to personal
problems, I am as muddle-headed as the worst of you, and
quite as impulsive and emotional and hopelessly undirected! " In his concern for the future of humanity, he
never lost his warm and abounding interest in humanity's
present pains and pleasures, with especial reference to the
manifold difficulties that surround the relations of the sexes.
This sympathy is the keynote of the group of novels published between 1896 and 1914. None is, strictly speaking,
autobiographical; yet each encloses large fragments of
personal experience; for, just as his Socialism began at
home, so did his understanding of human desires and
emotions. When re-reading these books, it is advisable to
keep open at one side the two volumes entitled *Experiment
in Autobiography*, and check the adventures of his imaginary
personages by the adventures of his own youth, from
Bromley High Street onwards. His reflections on Uppark,
and the place occupied by such relics of the past in the
existing social structure, are expanded at considerable length
in the pages of *Tono Bungay*, and the early effects of his
scientific training are analysed with immense care in the
brilliantly amusing story of *Love and Mr. Lewisham*. But
no less important is the experience supplied by his first and
second marriages. The emotional restlessness that always
characterised him, his own dependence on women and vague
persistent aspiration towards the perfect human relationship
which he somehow never quite achieved, also characterise Mr.
Lewisham and the heroes of *Tono Bungay* and *The New
Machiavelli*. At the moment, it would be neither permissible
nor discreet to inquire into the autobiographical foundation

175

of *The New Machiavelli* and *Ann Veronica*; but these books, it is pretty clear, possess a common basis, and there is little to choose between the elopement of Ann Veronica and her enamoured scientist, and that of the heroine of *The New Machiavelli* and her love-lorn politician. Each book has a " happy ending " that strangely fails to ring true.

Tono Bungay he once described as, in the field of novel-writing, probably his most ambitious effort. It is certainly the most delightful of the half-dozen important books published in that period; and its shortcomings—for it has many—are typical of the literary imperfections to be found in all the others. But let us begin upon the credit side. The central theme is brilliantly worked out, and interwoven with that theme are two memorable, sympathetic and closely detailed portraits—Edward Ponderevo, promoter and financier, and his wife, the narrator's aunt, who follows Ponderevo with quizzical devotion through his meteoric progress. In describing the adventurer himself, Wells would appear to have derived his inspiration from several different sources. There was the tragedy of Whittaker Wright, the fraudulent financier who killed himself behind the scenes at a London court of justice; and at the opposite end of the scale there was the astonishing career of Alfred Harmsworth, who concluded his career, rich and honoured, as a member of the House of Lords. Individually, they are not to be compared; but both exemplified the dazzling opportunities offered during the period of Wells's early manhood to men of ruthless drive and energy. Wells liked and admired Harmsworth; he recognised in him at last " a certain admirable greatness " and admitted that he had " travelled far from the mere headlong vulgarity of his first drive into prosperity." But he was alarmed by the almost unlimited power that, in the conditions of modern society, such an individual wielded, and by the contrast between " the real vastness of

the opportunities and challenges that crowded upon him . . .
and the blank inadequacy of his education " for other than
competitive aims. Harmsworth's success, according to
Wells, had caught him unaware and blown him sky high.
In Edward Ponderevo, he drew the portrait of a small man
boosted up to the heavens by tremendous accidental
opportunities, who flames there like an exploding rocket,
then hurtles down to earth again as a charred and extinguished stick. Ponderevo, the product of the new world,
is balanced by a portrayal of stately anachronistic Bladesover. Both are depicted with skill and gusto; but in neither
instance does he spoil the proportions of his narrative by
ramming home a theory. Ponderevo is never a type; and
" my aunt," who nags and loves, and laughs at him and
humours him, remains one of the more memorable creations
of the twentieth-century novel.

The weaknesses of *Tono Bungay*, on the other hand, are
startling and obvious. What perverse spirit induced the
novelist to attach to his main theme, first an irrelevant
adventure story—the account of how the narrator attempts
to retrieve his uncle's fortunes by stealing from a desert
island a hoard of some mysterious radio-active substance:
second, a love story as clumsy and unconvincing as it is
emotionally banal? Strange that H. G. Wells, the critic of
Bladesover, should let Bladesover beguile his imagination
with the vision of an aristocratic siren called " The Honourable Beatrice Normandy ": and that, having thoroughly
explored the same theme some years earlier in *Love and Mr.
Lewisham*, he should hark back to the disillusionments of an
early ill-adjusted marriage! Yet so it is: the general effect
of *Tono Bungay* is overloaded and top-heavy, and remains
an irritating mixture of the best and worst in Wells. Faults
of taste, errors of construction, appear in all our greatest
novelists. Wells's mistakes, on the other hand, are not merely

superficial, but are related both to his view of life and to his conception of the novelist's art. Thus, he wrote endlessly of love: but, owing to some failure of comprehension or lack of emotional delicacy—it was not sympathy he lacked or the desire to understand—his handling of the subject was often trite and vulgar. *Ann Veronica*, for example, is an absorbing but, in the last resort, eminently unsatisfactory volume. To-day, it has a vivid historical interest; the battle which it concerns had been won by 1918, and Ann Veronica's struggle with her father for the right to " lead her own life " seems now almost as remote as the struggle for parliamentary reform in the early nineteenth century. But, apart from its value as an historical document and the satirical glimpses of Fabian reformers and militant suffragettes, *Ann Veronica* has begun to show its age, while the idyllic episode with which it terminates has a saccharine vulgarity that sets the teeth on edge. Wells's lavish employment of three dots is nowhere more exasperating.

Kipps and *Mr. Polly*, on the other hand, are made of solider stuff than the runaway science student, since they crystallise an important aspect of the novelist's own character —his cocksureness and his humility, his persistent hopeful strivings towards a good and happy life, his refusal to conform or to be shoved by circumstances into the Procrustean bed of any established social category. He has been called the prophet of the Common Man; but one must add that it was the uncommonness of the Common Man that always most attracted him. He saw the ordinary man as a creature of soaring aspirations—usually stifled at birth— and of vast potentialities, which in ninety-nine cases out of a hundred were never fully realised. Perhaps he erred on the side of optimism. But then a tendency towards radical simplification was at once the weakness and the strength of Wells's intellectual methods. His literary imagination was bright but shadowless. It lacked a place for the finer and softer shades; it disdained, for example, the qualifications and reservations that lend so much to the beauty and variety of Henry James's life-work.

Moreover, Wells, despised humility. Brought up by his mother to be humble, to accept the dispensations of an all-wise Providence which had ordained Uppark and its house-keeper's room upon the one hand, Bromley High Street and its subterranean kitchen-living-room upon the other, he faced the world with perky self-assurance, stared it straight between the eyes and declined to take off his hat. Thus the religious emotions, though in middle life he produced an unfortunate book named *God the Invisible King*, were almost completely beyond the range of his sympathy and understanding. His greatest limitation, both as a novelist and a prophet, was a refusal to admit that his view might possibly be limited; for the essence of his gospel was a conviction that every problem could be solved—and solved immediately and permanently—if good will and a trained scientific intelligence were only brought to bear upon it. In the early, even in the middle books, there is still, vaguely apparent here and there, a lingering sense of mystery; but, after a certain period, the universe he surveyed contracted rather than expanded, and his belief in his own prophetic infallibility grew more and more insistent. He dismissed the experts, as he had dismissed the aesthetes, and in the *Outline of History* sought to reduce the whole recorded human past to the intellectual level of Kipps and Mr. Polly.

Yet there can be no doubt of the incalculable debt his contemporaries and successors owe him. " Wherever a young man, from the Arctic to the Tropics (wrote J. B. Priestley) was determined to free himself from mental squalor, fear, and ignorance, there was Wells at his side, eager to instruct, denounce, startle and inspire." Perhaps

" eager " is the most revelatory word. About him, even during old age, there was a disarming air of eagerness reflected in the brisk movements of his small, neat, grey-clad person and echoed in his high electrical squeak of a voice when he grew interested or excited. His was an exceedingly mercurial mind. " Although he would not have enjoyed being told so (continued Priestley's article) he had the temperament of an artist and not that of a scientist or a philospher." His mental processes were essentially intuitive; and, just as his prophetic preoccupations always tended to hamper his progress as an artist, so his artistic temperament made him a disseminator of ideas, a populariser of theories, rather than an original philosophic or scientific thinker. In his composition, the conflict between the artist and the journalist-propagandist, was never really settled. After two decades of increasingly tendentious work, during which the artist seemed to have sunk low indeed behind the literary horizon, he suddenly burst out, at the age of seventy-two, with that astonishing and disconcerting production, *Apropos of Dolores*, a novel without propagandist taint, in which the writer, angry as a boy at his first disappointed love affair, rails against the possessiveness of womanhood, its greed and its stupidity, through episode on ludicrous episode, and page on envenomed page.

Among unexpected products in an entirely different field, one must also mention the thesis he submitted towards the end of his life for a doctorate at an English university. Entitled *A Thesis on the Quality of Illusion in the Continuity of the Individual Life in the Higher Metazoa, with particular reference to the species Homo Sapiens*, this rare pamphlet seems calculated to undermine a great deal of Wells's previous teaching. If " there is not and never has been such an original mental unity " as is implied in the conception of self-hood, and if all " consolidations " of our personality are largely artificial, the idea of human perfectibility seems destined to go by the board, at least till the human organisation has reached a further state in its development. But, when this thesis was submitted, the shadows were already deepening. In one of his last published essays, Wells acknowledged a suspicion that the human race, having failed to adapt itself to its circumstances and surroundings, was an experiment that had failed and that, like other natural experiments, it would one day be superseded: that there was no issue from chaos: that no generation of *Men Like Gods* would ever arise on earth to justify his hopes and dreams: indeed, that only his nightmares, and not his dreams, were destined for realisation. The first atom bomb descended a year before his death; but during the twelve months that remained he had little taste for prophesying. He had helped to build a new world on the ruins of the nineteenth century, to open up new prospects—perhaps deceptive—of order, toleration, progress. He saw the insecurity of its hopeful foundations, and died, as in the midst of an earthquake, with the stable and civilised universe rocking all around him.

Sergeant Bourgogne and the Retreat from Moscow

ONCE AGAIN[1] the Beresina may be choked with corpses. Across the forests and plains through which Napoleon made his rapid and triumphant advance and his slow and calamitous withdrawal, between the June of 1812 and the January of 1813, rushes a tide, incomparably more gigantic, of blood and fear and suffering. Yet about the story of the retreat from Moscow there is a kind of dramatic completeness that still commands attention. Indeed, only by invocation of the tragic theory—by the supposition that a jealous God lies in wait for exceptional good fortune, and that *até* inevitably succeeds to *hubris*—can we quite explain the circumstances that led to Napoleon's greatest blunder. Those circumstances have been exhaustively (if inconclusively) discussed, and the development of the tragedy has often been recorded; but no record is more vivid than the Memoirs of Sergeant Bourgogne,[2] ex-*Grenadier-Vélite* of the Imperial Guard, who endured the worst horrors of the retreat and emerged with his belief in the Emperor's genius, and his devotion to his leader's memory, yet unshaken. His fascinating, at times appalling, narrative is a masterpiece of

[1] In 1941.
[2] *Memoirs of Sergeant Bourgogne.* With an introduction by Sir John Fortescue. The St. Giles Library. Cape.

untutored straightforward reporting, comparable to Diaz's story of the conquest of Mexico from which Prescott drew much of his most interesting material. Like the sixteenth-century Spanish adventurer, this middle-class Frenchman of the early nineteenth century was what nowadays, loosely and vaguely, we describe as an extrovert. The little we learn of his character we learn in spite of himself. Bourgogne was neither vainglorious nor sentimental. He did not sentimentalise his own sufferings or the sufferings of his comrades; he did not revolt against a world in which such catastrophes were possible, or against the imperial system to which they owed their immediate origin; he was content, quietly and simply, to chart the course of his adventures. Thus it had happened; thus his friends had died, frozen, burnt to death, sabred or speared by pursuing Cossacks; thus he had struggled home, with his scars and his loot, out of the Russian wilderness. He was delighted to remember: he did not attempt to analyse.

On one point he produces much curious evidence. The army that broke up along the road to Germany was already disorganised and demoralised before it had said good-bye to Moscow. Bourgogne was a good soldier and experienced campaigner, proud of his regiment, proud of the *Grande Armée*, proud of the splendiferous and resounding legend of which he felt he formed a part. But, in spite of the strict imperial order that forbade all plundering, he had begun to loot during his first day in the conquered city. Long before the ban was raised (as the conflagration caused by Russian incendiaries grew more and more extensive) the quarters he occupied were full of plunder and embellished by the presence of two female captives, whose services he retained until they were borrowed from him, good-humouredly but peremptorily, by Adjutant-Major Roustan. Life for non-commissioned officers of the Guard was a continual festivity;

and every evening they would gather in a deserted palace, there to recline " like pashas on ermine, sable, lion and bear skins, smoking costly tobacco in magnificent pipes," an enormous silver bowl before them filled with punch, above which slowly melted a huge loaf of sugar, held in place by a pair of captured Russian bayonets. No effort seems to have been made to save the army from the perils of this Capuan existence; and, when the Emperor decided to abandon the half-burnt but still habitable city, his troops were permitted to set forth in broken ranks, laden down with their booty, having many of them exchanged their uniforms, and even their arms and cartridge belts, for the silks and velvets they had picked up from Muscovite wardrobes. Bourgogne himself threw away his white full-dress trousers, " feeling pretty certain I should not want them again just yet," and carried a mere sixteen cartridges. Into his knapsack he had stuffed an amazing collection of objects, both perishable and precious:

. . . Several pounds of sugar, some rice, some biscuit, half a bottle of liqueur, a woman's Chinese silk dress, embroidered in gold and silver, several gold and silver ornaments, and amongst them a little bit of the cross of Ivan the Great. . . . A woman's large riding-cloak (hazel colour, lined with green velvet; as I could not guess how it was worn, I imagined its late owner to be more than six feet high), then two silver pictures in relief, a foot long and eight inches high; one of them represented the Judgment of Paris on Mount Ida, the other showed Neptune on a chariot formed by a shell and drawn by sea-horses, all in the finest workmanship. I had, besides, several lockets and a Russian prince's spitoon set with brilliants.

But that was not all:

I wore over my shirt a yellow silk waistcoat, wadded inside, which I had made myself out of a woman's skirt; above that a large cape lined with ermine, and a large pouch hung at my side . . . by a silver cord. This was full of various things—amongst them a crucifix in gold and a little Chinese porcelain vase.

His spirits were high. Confusedly, Bourgogne and his friends would appear to have imagined that the Emperor's plans still included the conquest of the Orient; and, as he left Moscow, he was already looking forward to the "Mongol, Chinese and Indian" mistresses whom he would undoubtedly acquire. On the 19th of October, the long garish procession got under way. There was rain on the 22nd, thick fog on the 25th; during the night of the 27th it began to freeze. Thereafter, the main outlines of the tragedy need no retelling. Bourgogne's story is memorable because it depicts the fortitude, the despair, the misery, the eventual triumph of a single, isolated, and often frightened, man. In addition to quick eyes, Bourgogne had that gift of cursory self-expression—of pinning down an episode in a line or a sentence—which is the despair of more practised and more ambitious writers. He saw much of pain—few men have seen so much in so brief a period—and his descriptions of human agony are as sympathetic as they are observant. The shapes assumed by death never ceased to horrify and interest him. Before the army had reached the Dnieper, dying men were being plundered as they lay in the snow:

I was walking now in a narrow footpath in the wood . . . and with me was one of my friends, a sergeant in the same regiment. We suddenly came upon a gunner of the Guard lying right across the path. By him was another gunner stripping his clothes from him. We could see

185

that the man was not dead, as his legs moved and every now and then he struck the ground with his fists.

So violent and so continuous was the pressure of self-interest, that some of the results it produced were almost comic. Near Smolensk, a huge barn crammed with eight hundred men suddenly caught fire. The doors were barricaded against late-comers; " cries and shrieks of rage were heard, the fire became a vast tossing mass, through the convulsive efforts the poor wretches made to escape." Meanwhile, from all around came running a horde of ragged, frozen and starving men. Some rifled the corpses they dragged from the blaze. Others observed cheerfully: " It serves them right . . ." " Others, again, stretched out their hands to the warmth saying, ' What a beautiful fire! . . .' "

Yet, although the retreat from Moscow had its grotesque and fantastic side—men with cracked lips and frost-bitten fingers fighting for the half-cooked flesh of broken-down horses; men devouring a few stolen potatoes in fearful stealth—through the squalor ran frequently a strain of splendour. With awe, Bourgogne witnessed the devotion of the hundred and fifty dragoons, who, the whole of one hideous winter night, stood massed in their long white cloaks around their hereditary chief, the young Prince Emile of Hesse-Cassel, " pressed tightly one against the other, protecting him from wind and cold. The next morning three-quarters of them were dead and buried beneath the snow. . . .' The examples of disinterestedness that he encountered were as startling, if not so numerous, as the instances of abject greed and savagery. There was the cavalryman whose first thought was always for the mount that had carried him in a dozen major actions; and there was the old sergeant of Bourgogne's regiment, named Daubenton who, league after league, supported on his back the regimental dog, when poor Mouton's paws were frost-bitten on the road to Wilna.

Bourgogne's narrative has something of that dream-like quality which we associate with states of intense physical exhaustion. The pictures he draws are vivid, but seen as it were through a slight transparent film. Again and again he protests his determination to be absolutely accurate—to put down the good and the bad just as he remembers them; and it is astonishing how capacious and retentive his memory proves. When he describes the fate of the three Russian ladies, who had been persuaded to accompany the retreat by a high French officer, he recollects in a flash the exact colour and trimming of the cloak one of them was wearing when he saw her dead body lifted from their foundered travelling carriage. He tells of losing his way at midnight beneath the walls of Smolensk; and back comes the reverberation of the mysterious organ music which had followed him like an obsession as he groped and stumbled through thick curtains of quietly falling snow. His method of narration is sometimes chaotic and fragmentary; but Bourgogne has an astonishing aptitude for evoking a broad panorama in very few words:

. . . We were roused by an extraordinary noise. This was the north wind travelling over the forests, bringing with it heavy snow and 27 degrees of frost, so that it became quite impossible for the men to stay where they had camped. We heard them shouting as they ran about towards any fire they saw; but the heavy snow storms caught them, and they could soon run no more, or if they tried to do so they fell and never rose again.

And, much later, as the survivors were approaching Kovno:

We heard at intervals the sound of the artillery, which seemed to us like the expiring sigh of our army.

It was by the death of the army as a collective organism, as much as by the fate of its individual members, that Bourgogne's imagination was most deeply troubled. His Memoirs are full of the love of the *Grande Armée*—its marching songs, its gallantries, its parade-ground slang, the *cantinières*, wrinkled or blooming, good humoured or morose, who had bumped along in their carts on the track of its victories and shared the grimmest moments of its dissolution. Bourgogne himself survived, not much the worse for wear till 1867, and during the forties, in a placid provincial hotel, he would sometimes recognise beneath the traits of a stout *commerçant* the comrade who had suffered with him in the snows of Russia. Then wives and families would be forgotten; wine would be drawn; and they would sit up far into the night, talking of this incident and that, and of how with their own eyes they had seen the Emperor, in fur-lined cloak and purple velvet cap, trudging, baton in hand, among the marshals and princes of the Empire. The Emperor—ah, what a mighty genius! how good to think and talk of him in the reign of the Citizen King! It is an odd fact that, although human beings may feel a transitory and selfish regard for the ruler who brings them prosperity and material contentment, it is to the leader who taxes their capacity for suffering and endurance that in after-years their imaginations and their hearts belong.

Civil Service

The family of Sanson

As CONSERVATIVE critics remind us, the family is the mainstay of France; and there is something particularly respectable about a family that continues in the same trade for several generations, gaining proficiency and adding to its distinction as the years go by. Father hands down his craft to son: children grow up among reminders of the hereditary calling that it is their pleasant lot to follow. Sad that such a succession should at length be cut short—as happened, for example, to the famous dynasty of the Sansons, a clan celebrated in the history of France from 1688 to 1847, when the last of the line was obliged to retire from office. The *Memoirs* of the family, published during 1862, describe his farewell in the course of a dramatic prologue: " On March 18th, 1847, I was returning home tired out after one of those long walks in which, among the loneliest surroundings I could discover, I sought to lose my gloomy reveries and the constant obsession of my spirit. Scarcely had I crossed my threshold and heard the old wicket-gate, so seldom opened, swing heavily shut behind me, squeaking on its rusty hinges, than the concierge handed me a letter. At once I recognised the massive seal—the seal that always made me shudder. . . . Arrived in my study I broke the fatal seal and tore the letter: IT CONTAINED MY DISMISSAL!!! A strange and

189

indefinable emotion possessed me. I lifted my eyes towards the portraits of my ancestors; I scanned their dark, meditative faces; I contemplated my grandfather, in hunting costume, leaning pensively on his gun, with one hand caressing his dog—perhaps the only friend his fate had ever given him."

How well the scene is set! With what art the writer conveys the impression of vague melancholy that hung about his forebears. Theirs and his had been an uncommon fate; they had inherited a profession that other and weaker men might not have envied (though the Sansons supported it with dignity and patience). They were, in fact, *Exécuteurs des Hautes œuvres de la Cour de Paris*, that is to say, public torturers and executioners whose business it was to inflict on criminals, both civil and political, the vengeance of society in the name of successive French governments. They had executed, to the accompaniment of appalling tortures, a distracted visionary, Damien, who attempted to assassinate Louis XV in 1757: they also beheaded, despite (we are asked to believe) many misgivings and considerable repugnance, the unlucky grandson of Louis XV in 1793.

They were devoted civil servants and, like all good civil servants, utterly impartial. Now and then, according to their *Memoirs*, one member of the family might faint and falter; but a brother, son or nephew was ready to take his place, manipulate the white-hot pincers or plunge the miscreant's hand into a dish of flaming sulphur, till justice had been done, the last shriek had died away and the final death-rattle had been extinguished. So History thundered on, and the dark-visaged, saturnine Sansons plodded grimly in its footsteps. Into their charge passed not only the famous and infamous, but an extraordinary assemblage of lesser-known victims: Madame Tiquet, " handsome, witty and accomplished," who had been convicted of several attempts to murder her aged husband, and who went to the scaffold radiant " in spotless white ": Cartouche, the formidable gangster, whose insolence and hardihood were so great that he counted " in a stentorian voice " the blows with which the executioner was breaking his limbs as he lay stretched upon the wheel. Damien was one of the strangest subjects that came their way, and his fate by far the most dreadful. No exact motive has been assigned to his unsuccessful attempt on the life of Louis XV; but he had revolutionary leanings and muddled religious beliefs, and seems to have conceived his desperate plan in a spirit of self-sacrifice. He failed, but the sacrifice was consummated amid torments as atrocious as, in the long history of human sadism, have ever been administered. The hand which had offended was literally burned off; the regicide's body was " *tenaillé*," or ripped with red-hot pincers, and into his wounds were poured boiling oil, molten lead, pitch and burning sulphur; he was then rent into four pieces by a team of sturdy horses. When Damien mounted the scaffold his hair was dark; when the remains of his corpse were assembled, onlookers noticed that his hair was snow-white. Readers of Casanova's autobiography will recollect that the Chevalier was lurking behind the scenes at Damien's execution, making love to his mistress of the moment, while she (but not her lover) watched the Sansons at work in the square beneath the window. . . .

Damien's was the last full-dress execution of the kind ever seen in Paris. It provided an opportunity for *macabre* description of which the author of the *Memoirs* took full advantage. More unexpected are the touches of human pathos. After he had suffered, during a preliminary investigation, the torture of the " Boot," Damien was observed to gaze at his mangled legs " *avec une espèce d'attendrissement douloureux* "; and, later, when they were

191

preparing to burn off his regicidal right hand, he examined it " *avec cette même expression de tristesse,*" as if he were bidding good-bye to an old and valued friend.

It is the tragedy of the civil servant's life that he is continually obliged to clean up after his superiors and to take the consequences of actions he has not himself approved. The Sansons had a decided conservative trend; but, ironically enough, it was an immense revolutionary upheaval that brought them in their biggest flow of business. Among the various events that may be said to have hastened the French Revolution, none was more remarkable than the fantastic confidence-trick, known as " The Affair of the Necklace," practised by Madame de la Motte and her husband on the fatuous Cardinal de Rohan, who was persuaded that he had captured the love of Marie-Antoinette. Madame de la Motte was convicted of fraud; and the fourth Sanson was ordered to superintend a public flogging, after which she was to be branded with a hot iron on both her shoulders. Madame de la Motte appeared to receive her sentence in a " silk *déshabillé,* striped brown and white, and covered with small nosegays of roses." During her punishment, she " never ceased shrieking," and, when the iron was applied to her naked shoulder, seized and bit a large morsel from the nearest assistant's hand.

The Affair of the Necklace opened the floodgates. Dr. Guillotin, aided by some hints he had received, through Charles Henri Sanson, from an ingenious " German engineer of the name of Schmidt," had perfected his celebrated machine by 1791. The conception was humanitarian: the condemned person, said Dr. Guillotin, addressing the assembled legislators of revolutionary France, would feel only " *a slight freshness on the neck* "; and the mechanically-minded King, who is reputed to have been one of the first to inspect the new device and discuss its possibilities, was among the first distinguished persons to put it to a practical proof. Thereafter the list is interminable: Charlotte Corday, smiling at the executioner as he pinioned her arms, with the words, " To be sure, you ought to know how to do it! ": the Queen, " her lips red, her eyes brilliant," followed to the scaffold by shouts of " Death to the Austrian! Death to Madame Veto! ": the scholarly Girondins and Madame Roland: Madame du Barry, a bloated relic of the reign of Louis XV, crying as Sanson had " never seen a woman cry before."

No wonder Charles Henri Sanson was known as " the great Sanson! " But his heyday ended: and the execution of Robespierre himself—half-conscious, his bullet-shattered jaw wrapped in a filthy linen bandage—initiated a far less profitable and more prosaic period. Meanwhile, the last of the Sanson line was receiving his education. The *Memoirs* have some touching stories to tell of the little boy's development—how, for example, he surprised his renowned grandfather in the garden looking at a row of bright crimson tulips and murmuring wistfully: " How fresh, how red they are! If they saw them, they would say that I water them in blood! " Before he retired, he had himself executed " over a hundred persons," but none of the same calibre as fell to his grandfather's share, and had become what he himself calls " an inactive spectator of executions," who took his stand on the scaffold as a matter of official form.

In 1847 the blow fell; the dynasty of the Sansons was brought to a sudden end; we are back again at the opening pages of the Sanson *Memoirs*, with their glimpse of a picturesque and gloomy personage taking a letter from his concierge, while the ancient wicket-gate groans on its rusty hinges. Unhappily we cannot remain there. One must add that the *Memoirs* were not quite the authentic document that their publishers pretended, but a compilation, made by a clever editor, at the instigation of an enterprising business man, who had bought his rights in the story from the last of the Sansons for the large sum of 30,000 francs. Henri Sanson had promised to supply notes and perhaps write the concluding volume, but (according to an article published in the *Temps* in 1875) he failed to keep his promise: he was an idle and extravagant old man, and his memory had weakened. Personally, he had the benevolent air of a decrepit *bourgeois*. He owed his dismissal to the fact that, having wasted his patrimony, he had been reduced to pledging the woodwork of the guillotine itself and, when summoned to perform his duty, was obliged to confess that his tools were not available. Asked how he had felt when his office made it necessary for him to take a human life, he reflected for some time and then replied, hesitantly: *"J'avais grand' hâte, monsieur, que ça fût fini"*—" I was in a great hurry, monsieur, to polish off the job."

Janus Weathercock

Or the Virtuoso's Tragedy

WE HAVE most of us contemplated committing a crime—
and wished that that particular crime could be committed
quietly, impersonally, without involving any danger of
detection. But the darkest intentions are not bad enough,
for to commit a crime one must traverse, or allow oneself
very gradually to drift across, a borderline that separates
wishful thinking from desperate acting, his "fashionably
dressed" audience from the man in the dock, ordinary
human beings from legendary monsters. The exact position
of this frontier-zone is hard to decide. Where does it begin?
Is there any point in his progress towards criminality at
which the criminal recognises that he has crossed the border
and that wild imaginings have assumed an uncomfortably
concrete shape? Or is the transition quite imperceptible?
Many celebrated felons have been habitual day-dreamers.
They are also—most of them—exceedingly conceited
persons, either armoured with an invincible self-righteous-
ness or intoxicated with their own intelligence and virile
bravado. Hauptmann (if we accept his guilt) was among the
former. "I feel I am innocent—I *am* innocent!" he is
reported to have exclaimed during the course of the long,
miserable, disgusting trial that sent him to the electric chair.
Landru was a member of the latter class, a small-time

swindler and petty amorist whose unconquerable egotism jutted like his famous beard. What pigeon-hole can we find for Thomas Wainewright, amiable virtuoso and accomplished poisoner, who graduated as a criminal from the half-world on the fringes of art?

To assign him a place, we must know something of the facts of Wainewright's ancestry. His maternal grandfather was Dr. Ralph Griffiths; and Dr. Griffiths, besides being the proprietor of the eminently respectable *Monthly Review* (on which he employed Oliver Goldsmith as a sweated assistant), was also the publisher of *Fanny Hill*, the most elegant of English pornographic novels. John Cleland obtained twenty guineas for his manuscript and, disappointed by his ill-success in the field of pornographic literature, turned to the philosophic study of language, producing a book entitled *The Way to Things by Words and to Words by Things*; but the publisher gathered in a handsome profit; and at the time of his death this " free-hearted, lively and intelligent " man, who " abounded beyond most men in literary history and anecdote," had managed to accumulate a fair-sized fortune and had bought himself a large house at Turnham Green. Linden House was strangely connected with Wainewright's destiny. The bookseller and publisher had become a gentleman; and the symbol of his gentility was an impressive building, secluded in its pleasant leafy gardens. Thomas Wainewright was determined to remain a gentleman, and aspired to the combined dignity of artist, author and Regency *bon viveur*.

By temperament, he was volatile, gay and expansive. " I am certainly an amiable creature " (he admitted in one of his occasional essays). " Every action of my life emanates from a wish to please." His friends, on the whole, agreed with this estimate. He was a " facetious, good-hearted fellow," remarked the rustic poet, John Clare. Barry

Cornwall spoke of his " restless pleasantry . . . ever veering, catching the sun and shade "; while Charles Lamb referred to him in print as " the light, and warm-as-light hearted Janus of the *London*." And, if he pleased his acquaintances, he pleased himself. Janus Weathercock—such was the pseudonym he had adopted—was the type of essayist who abounds in autobiographical whimsies and in agreeable reflections of his own good taste. He portrays himself in all manner of becoming attitudes. Now he is depicted driving up to London in his smart new gig, whisking " along green lanes, between high hedges of the sweet hawthorn and the elegant wild briar," peeping " betwixt the hazels at the dark blue scenery " or pausing to dabble his face " in a watery bed of cowslips, wet with May dews "; now he enumerates the graces of his cat and dog and faithful pet robin, his " scarlet-breasted pensioner," which " hops fearlessly along the smooth-rolled gravel walk," fixing " the gentle Janus," with its diamond-black eye; now he appears as a fashionable virtuoso whose " tables groan with the weight of volumes of Raffaelle, Michael Angelo, Rubens, Poussin, Parmegiano, Giulio, etc., etc.," whose outer rooms are embellished with " delicious, melting love-paintings " by Fuseli and whose inner sanctum is rich with ivories, Renaissance bronzes, blue silk draperies, buhl tables and " sweeping ottomans " in a Blessingtonian orgy of colours and modes. Amid these surroundings, Janus Weathercock loved to lie back and " read a good romance on a shiny day in February " or lapse by degrees " into that amiable sort of self-satisfaction, so necessary to the bodying out of those deliciously voluptuous ideas perfumed with languor, which occasionally swim and undulate, like gauzy clouds, over the brains of the most cold-blooded men." Wainewright was anything but cold-blooded. " Voluptuous " and " delicious " were adjectives for which he had a particular affection; and their demoralising influence creeps through his style. In Wainewright's prose, the maid-servant who attends him becomes immediately " a good-natured, Venetian-shaped girl "; the wine he drinks is a " flask of as rich Montepulciano as ever voyaged from fair Italia "; even the lamp sheds " a Correggio kind of light " which glows amorously on bibelots and gilt-tooled bindings.

Equally meretricious—with a hint of lubricity—were his drawings and water-colours. Wainewright had a lively erotic inventiveness but an extremely modest share of executive skill, which he had not improved by studying under Phillips, the romantic author of several portraits of Lord Byron. Yet one cannot deny him some scraps of talent. No doubt he could expand them in conversation till they seemed very much finer than indeed they were, for it is quite obvious that he imposed on the contemporary notables whom he assembled round him at his brilliant dinner-parties in Great Marlborough Street. These festivities helped to prepare his downfall. Wainewright had married in 1821— " a sharp-eyed, self-possessed woman dressed in showy, flimsy finery," who " obeyed his humours " and " assisted his needs," though " much affection did not apparently exist between them." Very soon the dashing couple were deep in debt. Faced with the prospect of being obliged to sell his grandfather's house (to which he felt a special and symbolic attachment), curtail his bibelot-buying and give up his luxuries, Wainewright discovered an ingenious alternative and set to work with pens and ink and tracing-paper. Five thousand pounds, left him by a Wainewright grandfather, were deposited in his name at the Bank of England. The capital, unfortunately, he could not touch; and Wainewright began by forging powers of attorney which enabled him to return the money to circulation. After all (he must have argued) it was *his* money! And what was a cleverly assumed signature, when executed by a man of fashion and taste? But his success stimulated Janus's mercurial brain. Towards the end of 1827 the Waine-wrights, again in difficulties, moved from London to the house at Turnham Green, accompanied by an uncle who was also a trustee. Six months later the old gentleman fell suddenly ill, developed convulsive symptoms and died in the agonies of strychnine poisoning.

He was followed, in 1830, by Wainewright's mother-in-law. Her agonies were as violent and as inexplicable as those of George Griffiths; but no inquiries were made into her death, and Wainewright, who had profited by her dis-appearance to the extent of a much-needed hundred pounds, was now at liberty to prepare his final *coup*. Its instrument and victim was his wife's half-sister, Helen Abercromby, a dull and unattractive young woman, who enjoyed bouncing health and had complete faith in her worldly relatives. By them she was induced to visit a number of insurance offices, sign false declarations and insure her life for a period of two years and a total sum of £16,000. Later she transferred these policies to Wainewright and, later still, was persuaded by Wainewright, after a visit to the play, to consume an injudicious midnight meal, which consisted of oysters and bottled porter. That night she complained of sickness and a "restless headache." The Wainewrights nursed her devotedly, but Helen died.

So concluded Weathercock's career as a poisoner. Strychnine and antimony are thought to have been the poisons that he employed—drugs of which the effects were then but imperfectly understood; the post-mortem yielded negative results, and, had it not been for the obstructiveness of the insurance companies, Wainewright's speculation might have brought him in a dividend. But the companies adopted a truculent attitude. Harassed by his creditors, unable to collect the profits of Helen's death, Wainewright was obliged to cross the Channel and vanish into an indigent and haunted obscurity. What he did—how he lived—we do not know. It was not till 1837 that he emerged from the shadows of Continental exile, returned on some unhappy impulse to England and was observed by a policeman " talking to a female, near a lamp, in Howland Street, Fitzroy Square." He was clapped into Newgate and committed for trial. Even so, he was not put on trial for murder —the murders, though strongly suspected, were never brought home; he was tried for his forgeries of fifteen years earlier and for them sentenced to transportation to Van Diemen's Land. Of Janus Weathercock's existence at an Antipodean convict station, during a period when Australian and Tasmanian prison-settlements rivalled the worst horrors of French Guiana and the American chain-gang system, comparatively little can now be gathered. Somehow he struggled through the rigorous probationary stage and, during later years, was permitted to eke out a livelihood by doing feeble sketches of the local officials and gentry. But at the same time, he produced a curious self-portrait, with the caption: " Head of a *Convict*, very characteristic of low *cunning* and *revenge*! "

Neither the face nor the expression is reassuring—a down-at-heel Mephistopheles, with tilted eyebrows, sharp beady pupils, foxy moustache and drooping hair. Thus Macready and Dickens must have seen him when, on a conducted tour around Newgate with Dickens's illustrator, the other members of the party were startled by a cry from Macready: " My God! there's Wainewright! " " In the shabby genteel creature, with sandy disordered hair and dirty moustache, who had turned quickly round at our entrance, looking at once mean and fierce. . . . Macready had been horrified to recognise a man familiarly known to

him in former days, and at whose table he had dined."
Here Wainewright's defiance is perhaps slightly more engaging than Macready's ingenuous consternation, Dickens's
literary zest or Forster's moral humbug. Wainewright was
a peculiarly atrocious criminal; but it is interesting to
discover once again how close is the connection between
criminality and the ordinary acquisitive human instincts,
and how slight and vague is the dividing line that appears
to separate them. A recent biography[1] has helped to
abolish the romantic legend woven round Wainewright's
name by Oscar Wilde, and later re-vamped by Dr. Mario
Praz, author of *The Romantic Agony*. For Wilde, Janus
Weathercock was a highly cultured, amusingly perverted
aesthete; for Dr. Praz, he is a literary sadist in the grand
tradition. Plainly, he was neither one thing nor the other,
but a sort of Harold Skimpole who resorted to poisoning,
as Skimpole himself might have resorted to card-sharping,
without the smallest loss of his interior self-esteem. In spite
of everything, he was still a gentleman and a man of feeling.
It was the custom at Newgate, he remarked, for cell-mates
to take turns in sweeping their out cell; his companions were
a bricklayer and a sweep; " but, by God, they never offer me
the broom! " At the same time, it entertained him to shock
his visitors; and, interrogated as to how he could have had
" the cold-blooded barbarity to kill such a fair, innocent, and
trusting creature as Helen," he replied with characteristic
jauntiness: " Upon my soul, I don't know, unless it was
because she had such thick ankles." Worse reasons have
been advanced for killing more attractive and intelligent
women; Janus Weathercock offers an impregnable surface
to praise or blame. If there was one faculty he lacked, it
was that of self-criticism. If there was one weakness that

[1] *Janus Weathercock.* The Life of Thomas Griffiths Wainewright. By
Jonathan Curling. Nelson.

especially distinguished him, it was an unconquerable self-love—a determination that the vulgar world should allow him his due. Poor Janus, why shouldn't he have inherited a fortune? And what a good thing that we are most of us inveterate cowards!

Chinese Poetry

" *Ça pue la merde et la mort,*" said a travelled friend of the
Goncourts whom they had asked for his impressions of a
journey through the Chinese Empire. It is a remark that
must have occurred to many later travellers, overlooking
some vast tawny northern plain, naked and dusty in the
bright spring sunshine, but raised and roughened as far as
the eye could reach with innumerable grave-mounds: when
they passed row after row of the conical brick ovens in
which a provident peasantry stores up its waste products, or
stopped their noses against the strangely mingled odours of
a Chinese town or village. To pay even the briefest visit
to an ancient Chinese city, drive through its winged gates
into the adjacent countryside and stand momentarily upon
the fringe of the gigantic hinterland, is an imaginative
experience of the kind that only travel furnishes. You have
an idea of distance beyond distance, of mountain-screen
behind mountain-screen and of valley succeeding valley,
every crumbling acre toiled over and treasured by the blue-
smocked inhabitants of uncounted mud-walled villages,
patiently digging and manuring till they are themselves dug
in. . . . The Chinese landscape seems an enormous vacuum,
and you, the traveller, poised on its edge, solitary and
insignificant as, except in instants of deep physical and
nervous dejection, you have never felt before.

You may remember then how De Quincey, whose knowledge of China was limited to travellers' tales, declared that
merely to think of the country and its people depressed and
terrified him. Since De Quincey's day, a host of Western
scholars and explorers have helped to clarify our understanding of the Chinese background, and have demonstrated,
for example, that what was once considered the flower of
Chinese art and craftsmanship—the scroll-paintings, jades
and lacquers of the age of Ch'ien Lung—was, in fact, the
debased offshoot of a declining civilisation. Modern
research has given us some superficial acquaintance with
the incomparable achievements of the T'ang and Sung
dynasties; it has excavated the bronzes and the carvings of
Han, and has photographed magnificent works of monu-
mental sculpture. Yet China's contribution to our world
heritage, for the average educated Westerner, remains
extremely enigmatic. His mind cannot compass such a
tremendous expanse of years: he is astonished by the
persistent vitality of the Chinese people, yet baffled by the
strain of rigid intellectual conservatism that, at least until
the fall of the Manchu dynasty, pervaded many aspects of
their culture. His own inheritance is revolutionary. He is
conscious of his personal debt to the past; but every century
he can look back on has brought with it some violent and
far-reaching upheaval in thought and art and manners. In
the East, it may strike him, the past assimilates the present:
Chronos perpetually devours his children: Athena springs
from the head of Jove, only to sink back again.

Nor are these misgivings the property of the West alone.
Reading the books of modern Chinese intellectuals, anxious
to persuade us that a contemporary panacea is now in
process of being applied to all the ancient evils, I seem to
detect an attitude towards the past both reluctantly respect-
ful and unconsciously apprehensive. Thus Lin Yutang,

describing his visit to a thriving Kuomintang stronghold, wrote—with veneration but also, I felt, with a certain hesitation—of the immense relics of the vanished city of Ch'ang-an that lie just beyond its purlieus. Yes, there is too much of the past in China; its characteristics are too deeply engrained, too alien from his own traditions and inherited way of thinking, for the ordinary Westerner to digest with any comfort. Only art provides an occasional release. Suddenly from flaking scroll or green-encrusted vessel glimmers an assurance that, although human races are vastly different, between the minds of individual artists there are unnumbered points of contact. The ruins of Ch'ang-an are largely unexplored; but a reader can turn to the English renderings of poems composed when that deserted site was a great imperial metropolis, alive with scholarly officials, and the resort of famous poets, whose sensibility responded to the emotions that underlie all poetic literature, and who translated their response into elaborate literary forms that are still comprehensible and still profoundly moving.

Many years have passed since Arthur Waley published his first volume of translations from the Chinese. At the time there was a murmur of criticism, mostly unintelligent. How much, we were asked, did the charm of these renderings owe to the translator? Across the gulf of more than a thousand years, how authentic was the echo of Po Chü-i's voice? Was not Chinese poetry a kind of sleight-of-hand? —the last a suggestion made with such blustering emphasis by one well-known Georgian poet that Mr. Waley (it is related) silently handed his critic a sheet of paper and a pencil, and handed back the result, when he had examined it, as gravely and courteously, but no less silently. Japanese critics, on the other hand, who, unlike Mr. Waley's victim, were equally familiar with English and Chinese verse, have informed me that, although they did not always agree with the English translator's choice of *vers libre* as a medium, they could not quarrel with his accuracy or dispute his scholarship. And then, scholarship apart, these versions possess a distinguishing trait that could not fail to recommend them—Arthur Waley is a poet in his own right; he handles free verse easily and gracefully as it has been handled by few other modern writers.

No previous or subsequent translator has quite attained to Arthur Waley's standard. Under his direction, as in one of those panoramic Chinese pictures where, between drifts of cloud, the red eaves of a palace or temple, a crag, a foaming torrent, a terraced hillside, emerge in a series of brief and brilliant glimpses, we gain an impression, fragmentary but vivid, of two thousand years of literature. Here are folk-songs from the *Book of Odes*, written before the time of the Persian attack on Greece, and poems by Li Po, Tu Fu and Po Chü-i, scholars, officials and men of the world, who flourished in the eighth and ninth centuries. Of the three, Po Chü-i seems from the Western point of view most immediately sympathetic. To compare different arts, and poets who spring from different races and different periods, is always somewhat dangerous. But there are occasions when Po Chü-i would appear to be very close to Herrick (a far more robust and original poet than is usually suspected); while his absorption in, and identification of himself with, the scene he is describing, recall the Sung landscape-painters, brought up in the school of Tao. Not that Po Chü-i is a wholly impersonal poet. The great majority of his poems begin in the first person singular: he is sad or tired or nostalgic; he is growing bald and growing old and remembers the friends he has left behind in the courts of the imperial city. But the customary effect of his verses is to lead the reader's mind from sensations that are personal to emotions that are general, till " I " has merged and dissolved in the mood of time and place.

Just as captivating—and perhaps more stimulating— are poets of an earlier epoch. " During the Han dynasty (wrote Robert Trevelyan[1]) between 206 B.C. and A.D. 220, when China was emerging from a feudal and semi-barbaric society into a more stable and cultured civilisation, a number of poems were written, which in style and subject-matter were very different from the classical types. They were composed not in symmetrical stanzas, but in irregular verses of changing character. . . . They often show a vigour and breadth of imagination unlike anything else in Chinese literature." For instance, he cites a poem entitled " The Bones of Chuang Tzu," by Chang Hêng (A.D. 78-139), which, he declares, " need not fear comparison with Lucretius and Leopardi. . . ." That it is an astonishing work there can be be no question, at least in the energetic guise that Mr. Waley lends it. His employment of the English language is always supple and ingenious; translating Po Chü-i, he achieves rhythmic effects of unusual pliancy and smoothness well suited to that poet's peculiar literary temperament; but in this poem he strikes out into far stormier, more dramatic measures. The protagonist has embarked on some interminable nightmare journey, through the " Nine Wilds " and the " eight continents," across " red deserts," and " northward waded through the wintry burghs of Yu ":

And now with rearing of rein-horse,
Plunging of the tracer, round I fetched
My high-roofed chariot to westward.
Along the dykes we loitered, past many meadows,
And far away among the dunes and hills.

From the Chinese. Edited by R. C. Trevelyan. Oxford Press.

Suddenly I looked and by the road-side
I saw a man's bones lying in the squelchy earth
Black rime-frost over him; and I in sorrow spoke
And asked him, saying, " Dead man, how was it?
Fled you with your friend from famine and for the last grains
Gambled and lost? Was this earth your tomb,
Or did floods carry you from afar? Were you mighty, were
*   you wise,*
Were you foolish and poor? A warrior or a girl? "

The living speaker offers to pray for the dead man's resurrection:

The dead man answered me:
" O Friend, how strange and unacceptable your words! . .
Of the Primal Spirit is my substance; I am a wave
In the river of Darkness and Light.
The Maker of All Things is my Father and Mother,
Heaven is my bed and earth my cushion,
The thunder and lightning are my drum and fan . . .
Wash me and I shall be no whiter,
Foul me and I shall yet be clean.
I come not, yet am here;
Hasten not, yet am swift."
The voice stopped, there was silence.
A ghostly light
Faded and expired.

It would have been a bold prophet who, confronted with these lines or with " The Great Summons," by Ch'ü Yüan of the fourth century B.C. ventured to predict the later development of Chinese classical verse. The art and literature of T'ang and Sung, a Western critic may feel, at the period of their most exquisite flowering had begun to disclose a hint of the weaknesses that would finally undermine them. Every extreme refinement of sensibility must one day overreach itself. The culture that spreads too far will eventually spread too thin; and, even more dreadful for a poet than living in a world where nobody reads or professes to enjoy poetry, is to be the member of a society where everybody writes it. Should the educated classes write and criticise verse as part of their official duties, then the poet's doom is sealed; for nothing is so inimical to the artist's creative gift as a civilisation that, instead of discarding inherited standards of taste (as happened in Europe after the Industrial Revolution), preserves certain vestiges of a traditional sense of style, unsupported by the imaginative vitality that gives taste and a sense of style their true aesthetic value. Such, at different times, has been the predicament of the civilisations built up by Japan and China. Such is the problem that faces modern Chinese poets. The efforts they have made to solve it, and their desperate attempts to reconcile the rival claims of past and present ages, are illustrated in the sheaf of poems, graceful and allusive yet strangely insubstantial, with which the editor of *From the Chinese* has elected to conclude his book.

English Devotional Verse

DEVOTIONAL LITERATURE flourishes on doubt, as love upon jealousy. In a period of serene and unruffled faith we may imagine a succession of patriarch pietists, seated like Blake's Job each under his own oak tree, striking their harps and raising their voices in solemn thanksgiving: but we cannot conceive of a Donne, a Traherne, a Hopkins. Religious verse is seldom the statement of assured belief but more often the passionate protestation of a mind that wishes to believe and believes and doubts again. It is the record of Jacob's conflict with his immortal adversary. Thus, the periods most prolific of devotional masterpieces are those in which a certain body of religious faith is counterbalanced by a definite strain of inquietude. The stage must have been set for a spiritual conflict; and, if the Elizabethan heyday did not add to its poetic achievements the production of great religious verse, it was because the two elements in the Elizabethan character—the devotional and the sceptical, the medieval and the modern—had not yet quite had an opportunity of coming to grips. On the one hand there is the paganism of Marlowe, the profound scepticism of Shakespeare's later tragedies; on the other, those vestiges of superstition, that terror of death and dread of the after-life, which haunt the work of Shakespeare's predecessors like the tolling of a plague-bell:

Wit with his wantonness
Tasteth death's bitterness;
Hell's executioner
Hath no ears for to hear
What vain art can reply;
I am sick, I must die—
   Lord, have mercy on us!

Yet it was a man brought up among the Elizabethans who rose to become one of the greatest of English religious poets, a profane and sensual versifier who, having in the sixteenth century earned himself a fashionable reputation as the author of witty and " conceited " love lyrics, emerged in the next as a master of religious eloquence. Hardly less remarkable than the mysterious inner metamorphosis that transformed the poet of " *Les Illuminations* " and " *Un Saison en Enfer* " into the unsuccessful trader and amateur gun-runner known as Harar in the cities of the Red Sea, was the spiritual revolution that swept over Donne. Yet both Rimbaud and Donne were strangely consistent. At his most profligate, Donne had envisaged love as subject for ruthless personal experimentation in which he delved more and more energetically:

Some that have deeper digg'd loves Myne than I,
Say, where his centrique happinesse doth lie:
   I have lov'd, and got, and told,
But should I love, get, tell, till I were old,
I should not find that hidden mysterie;
   Oh, 'tis imposture all. . . .

And, just as in love he had pursued not so much a temporary satisfaction as a " centrique happinesse " that perpetually eluded him

So, lovers dreame a rich and long delight,
But get a winter-seeming summer's night . . .

the penitent attacked faith with a lover's ardour and wooed
and invoked it with all the ingenuity at a lover's command.

Donne's "*Holy Sonnets*" were written soon after the
death of Ann Donne, during a period of black spiritual
depression, at a time when, according to his earliest biographer, he abjured every hope of earthly comfort and
"betook himself to a most retired and solitary life." Their
effect is as ominous and oppressive as the mood that begot
them. Doubt is the gloomy background against which faith,
or the aspiration towards faith, performs its dazzling
acrobatics. And doubt is made darker by fear of death—
by fear of the unknown, an absorbing fear of the Deity:

Thou hast made me, And shall thy worke decay?
Repaire me now, for now mine end doth haste,
I runne to death, and death meets me as fast,
And all my pleasures are like yesterday;
I dare not move my dimme eyes any way,
Despaire behind, and death before doth cast
Such terrour, and my feeble flesh doth waste
By sinne in it, which it t'wards hell doth weigh. . . .

Fitfully and far away, salvation glimmers. He is as lost and
helpless as once in the clutches of physical love.

Characteristic of Donne is the curious honesty with
which he is perpetually harking back to memories of
amorous torment and worldly satisfaction:

No, no; but as in my idolatrie
I said to all my profane mistresses . . .
. . . So I say to thee . . .

and the intense intellectual effort with which he appears to hammer out his poems line by line. The harshness and difficulty of many passages (deprecated alike by Jonson, who observed that although Donne was " the first poet in the world, *in some things*," for " not keeping of accent " he deserved hanging, and by Augustan critics who decided that all that Donne needed to become a really good poet was reinvestiture in flowing classical measures) are to-day a positive recommendation and, by contrast, heighten the effect of his flashes of eloquence. Donne is the least literary of devotional poets, but the most fascinating, the most complicated and the most persuasive.

Very different from the turbulent mysticism of the Dean of St. Paul's, expressed so often in images of violence and suffering—

> *Batter my heart, three person'd God; for, you*
> *As yet but knocke, breathe, shine, and seeke to mend;*
> *That I may rise, and stand, o'erthrow mee, and bend*
> *Your force, to breake, blowe, burn and make me new . . .*

was the calm and collected piety of George Herbert (a more accomplished technician though a lesser poet) whose relations with the Deity, despite the moments of doubt and acute despondency that even he did not escape, were as harmonious and as productive of happiness as those of Donne were argumentative and overshadowed. For Donne, God is the stern taskmaster, the supreme enigma; for Herbert, the welcome guest and familiar friend, a projection of the subtlety and charm of his own intelligence. In his moments of rebellion, Herbert remains the divine who had been a dandy and a cultured courtier:

> *I know the ways of Pleasure, the sweet strains,*
> *The lullings and the relishes of it;*
> *The propositions of hot blood and brains;*
> *What mirth and music mean; what Love and Wit*

Have done these twenty hundred years and more;
I know the projects of unbridled store;
My stuff is flesh, not brass; my senses live,
And grumble oft that they have more in me
Than He that curbs them, being but one to five:
      Yet I love Thee.

and it is typical of the devotional literature of the seventeenth century that poets should bring to it all the resources of worldly experience and refuse to be limited by any of the conventions of religious versifying.

Vaughan and Traherne are as sophisticated in expression as they are unworldly in sentiment. Intimations of immortality are discovered, not only with the help of prayer or during spells of intense spiritual absorption, but among the ordinary occurrences of the day-to-day life. Passion itself is sifted for its devotional residue, and love of the Creator is skilfully sublimated from love of the creature. Vague desires, restless longings and unfocused impulses receive a new, devout direction in the poet's mind:

    For giving me desire,
An eager thirst, a burning ardent fire,
    A virgin infant flame,
A love with which into the world I came,
    An inward hidden heavenly love,
    Which in my soul did work and move,
    And ever me inflame,
With restless longing, heavenly avarice,
    That never could be satisfied,
    That did incessantly a Paradise
Unknown suggest, and something undescried
Discern, and bear me to it; be
Thy name for ever praised by me.

That spiritual curiosity and " heavenly avarice," that persistent, almost greedy, search for an unknown Eden, is the inner theme of all seventeenth-century religious literature.

Yet, on this central theme, the variations are numerous and brilliant and, while Donne is moody and impassioned, Herbert finely eloquent, Vaughan delicately lyrical, Traherne an inquisitive searcher after that condition of perfect spiritual happiness which he imagined that he had glimpsed in his childhood but never found again, Crashaw imports the splendours of the Counter-Reformation and develops his English piety into patterns of baroque magnificence. The effect of his verse is both intoxicating and, in the end, a little cloying. Erotic and religious symbolism have seldom been more innocently yet wildly confused. The ascetic Fellow of Peterhouse, renowned for the austerity of his nightly vigils but expelled from his college by Puritan inquisitors, discovered in the Roman Church all the colour and warmth he needed and consumed himself in a blaze of sensuous devotionalism:

> *Like a soft lump of incense, hasted*
> *By too hot a fire, and wasted*
> *Into perfuming clouds, so fast*
> *Shalt thou exhale to heaven at last*
> *In a resolving sigh, and then*
> *O what? Ask not the tongues of men.*

His religious love-poems are as exquisite as they are disconcerting and lack the slightly saccharine quality of Coventry Patmore. Certainly they could have been written at no other period.

So much for a few, and then only the more conspicuous and better-known, figures of an epoch when every versifier was a religious poet and many minor poets achieved their greatest successes in the religious field. Milton has been omitted as a writer too large, too various, and too complex for cursory examination. But we have also omitted smaller contemporaries—Henry More, that enigmatic Platonist, admired by Coleridge and Lamb, whose " Song of Bathynous " often approaches, though it never quite attains to, poetic sublimity; William Habington, country gentleman and " spoiled Jesuit "; John Norris, author of " The Aspiration," which deserves a place in any anthology of religious poems; Quarles, whose over-elaborate imagery is set off, now and then, with real grace and freshness; Edward Sherburne, who, on the subject of St. Mary Magdalen, produced verses in the finest tradition of metaphysical ingenuity:

The proud Egyptian queen, her Roman guest,
(To express her love in height of state and pleasure)
With pearl dissolved in gold, did feast,
　　Both food and treasure.
And now, dear Lord, thy lover, on the fair
And silver tables of thy feet, behold!
Pearl in her eyes, and in her hair
　　Offers thee gold.

Sherburne survived till 1702; and it was during the century whose opening years he lived to see that the flow of English religious verse began to dwindle, and was diverted into tamely conventional courses. Pope's few religious efforts, and those passages of the " Essay on Man " where his own belief appears to predominate over Bolingbroke's Deism, are among the least distinguished works he ever produced; and, if we except the lamentations of the hell-obsessed Cowper and the imposing, if redundant, fervour of Christopher Smart, there remains little else but Watts and the brothers Wesley. It is questionable whether Watts (hampered by a reputation for terrific didacticism and

pursued by the parodies of Lewis Carroll) has ever received
his poetic due. His ode on " The Day of Judgment,
Attempted in English Sapphick," is a magnificently spirited
piece of work and reminds us that, although Isaac Watts
died in 1748, he was born in 1674. But his achievement
pales beside that of the Wesleys; and, were one called upon
to produce from the Augustan Age a poem worthy of the
devotional genius of an earlier period, it is to Charles
Wesley one would go to supply the omission:

> *Come, O Thou Traveller unknown,*
> *Whom still I hold, but cannot see,*
> *My Company before is gone,*
> *And I am left alone with Thee,*
> *With Thee all Night I mean to stay,*
> *And wrestle till the Break of Day.*
>
> *I need not tell Thee who I am,*
> *My Misery, or Sin declare,*
> *Thyself hast call'd me by my Name,*
> *Look on thy Hands, and read it there,*
> *But who, I ask Thee, who art Thou,*
> *Tell me thy Name, and tell me now?*

Here is something of that eloquence and that troubled
fervour which we distinguish in the work of Crashaw and
Donne, though the expression of it is less elaborate and less
elusive. Here, too, are a moral energy and a devout direct-
ness that seem to anticipate the great religious poets of the
nineteenth century.

" This is the Way the World Ends . . . "

THERE IS[1] a great deal to be said for the kind of book that, although itself it may be possessed of no particular aesthetic value, gives free play to the literary imagination. For instance, that absorbing and, in spite of the remoteness of the period it covers, strangely topical production, Samuel Dill's *Roman Society in the Last Century of the Western Empire*, a work one often takes up and often puts down again, on so many long digressions does it start the fancy. One returns home from these expeditions baffled and yet stimulated. Comparable only to the oddity of the present age is the oddity of the two turbulent, disastrous centuries when the Roman Empire, afflicted by some disease of which no historian has yet provided an altogether satisfactory diagnosis, sickened and slowly collapsed on a belated deathbed. The process of decline was majestically gradual. There were whole generations—and during the entire period of dissolution there were large and highly civilised communities—to whom the tragedy of the age they lived in was never apparent. Most human beings, luckily for themselves, are unimaginative. Indeed, to the various explanations of the fall of the Western Empire that have already been produced, one might add another—that Rome expired,

[1]Written in 1939.

218

not of the disruptive influence of Christianity; not, as one was taught to believe at school, of sheer moral weakness, for the " moral tone " of the period was often uncomfortably high; but of a sort of intellectual complacency that froze its life-blood. Nothing could shake the Roman faith in the Roman system. Though Alaric had so far prevailed against his own superstitious reverence for the idea it incorporated, as to capture and pillage the sacred city, his act of impiety was generally ignored or speciously explained away—except, of course, by the gloomier type of Christian ascetic. The cultured patricians and fashionable *littérateurs* of Gaul and Italy continued to uphold the grand tradition of their Imperial past.

A curious numbness seems to have crept over the contemporary intellect. " The Roman world (said a Christian) went laughing to its death." But, though it is true that the burghers of Cirta and Carthage were loudly encouraging their favourite charioteers while the armies of the Vandals attacked their walls, and that " the leading citizens of Treves . . . were revelling in a frenzy of drunken debauchery" on the eve of their annihilation by a barbarian horde, for a broad laugh—at least, among the patrician classes—should be substituted the image of a gentle smile, grave, condescending, remotely superior. Especially fascinating in Dill's monograph are the portraits that he draws of the cultured and leisured aristocrats of the fourth and fifth centuries, who, living, as it now appears, in conditions of general misery and unparalleled social chaos, still enjoyed the advantages of their birth and education upon immense and beautiful estates above the Rhône or Garonne. Culture was theirs—without the impetus that makes culture creative. It is as if the imagination of these Silver Age scholars, sapped by the cultural in-breeding of so many centuries, had become incapable of extension beyond a certain point, so that the true magnitude of contemporary events entirely escaped them. Thus, Symmachus, writing to his son in 402, the year of the great battles of Pollentia and Verona, makes no allusion to the presence of invaders, but " confines himself to the bare announcement of the fact that, owing to the unsafe state of the roads, he has had to make a long detour to reach the Court of Milan." Later, the same elegant rhetorician, a member of that conservative pagan or quasi-pagan aristocracy which put up a last determined stand for the old beliefs, merely indicates the confusion that prevailed by observing that he is " debarred . . . by the prevalence of brigandage " from enjoying the beauties of a particular country seat, one of fifteen he owned in various parts of Italy. Similarly, more than half a century later, Apollinaris Sidonius of Auvergne, when he is summoned by the Emperor from Gaul to the Court, reveals in the letters that describe his journey an enthusiastic preoccupation with the mythological and historical reminiscences it aroused in his mind—the sisters of Phaethon weeping their amber tears into the waters of the Po, the melodious memory of Virgil's Tityrus—but gives no hint of the appalling and critical contests of which Northern Italy had been the scene during the last fifty years. Arrived in Rome, he devotes his attention to verse and visiting, comments on the gaiety of the decaying metropolis, but betrays no knowledge that, only twelve years earlier, Rome had been despoiled by the Vandals and Berbers for nearly a fortnight, and that many of its chief treasures were destroyed or stolen. Rome was the moribund centre of a broken-down system; its statues would soon be more numerous than its human inhabitants; but for Sidonius the advance of twilight was very slow, and a sunset glory still hung round the Capitol and Palatine, though the roofs of temples and palaces had lost their gold.

Had Sidonius been a really perceptive pessimist, how

memorable a book he might have written! As it is—since he saw the present day only in tiny fragments, each fragment surrounded and softened by the glow of the past—the records he left are usually vague and disappointing. True, there is his vivid description of the Court of Theodoric, and, scattered up and down his voluminous letters, with their debased Latin and too-elaborate use of antithesis, there are some random appreciations of barbarian rule. The invaders were not necessarily brutal task-masters. They had entered the Empire, many of them, by invitation; even the Huns had battled for Rome as mercenaries; and it was by their uncouthness rather than by their treachery or ferocity that Romans of the period were chiefly offended. Impossible quite to assimilate them in the Roman picture—the Burgundians, good humoured and well-intentioned, who had a horrid practice of greasing their hair with rancid butter and after banquets (which sensitive Roman dignitaries occasionally found it expedient to attend) indulged in interminable drunken, raucous sing-songs; the swift-footed Herulians, whose cheeks were tattooed a bright bluish-green " like the colour of the waves "; the Gothic elders clad in tunics of wild beasts' skins barely reaching to the knees; the idolatrous, blue-eyed Saxon pirates and the shaven Franks! Humiliating that it should be necessary to coax and flatter them! Worse still to observe that, in Rome itself, the modes of these ridiculous, if gallant and serviceable, outsiders were sometimes adopted by citizens born! And at the end of the fourth and beginning of the fifth centuries the hard-worked Emperor Honorius was obliged to issue no less than three angry edicts, to prohibit within the precincts of the imperial city such barbarian fashions as long hair, trousers, and fur overcoats.

But if the social scene was changing, so was the terrestrial landscape. The great open cities of the Antonine age, planned on a scale of spacious magnificence with temples and triumphal arches and theatres and baths, were being rebuilt haphazard as fortified townships. The materials of their walls were quarried from earlier buildings, and within those walls a new town-life had come into existence—cramped, squalid, insanitary and fearful, an expression of the misery endured by a hopelessly impoverished proletariat and a ruined disintegrating middle class. Out of the Italy of Hadrian and Marcus Aurelius was emerging that " picturesque " Italy of Salvator Rosa and Piranesi which did not wholly vanish till the Risorgimento—a land of ruined aqueducts, roofless basilicas and weedy grottos, where shepherds and brigands pitched their camps among the fallen columns and broken architraves of derelict imperial dwellings, and necromancers held their conjurations in the Colosseum. What fate overtook the elegant villa-dwellers? During the sixth century a number of the old aristocratic Gallo-Roman families still managed to retain their original possessions and continued to exist on friendly terms with their barbarian neighbours. After that? But the darkness was slowly thickening. Odd to think of the dispersion and decay of those huge libraries—to imagine the day (for, however gradual the course of history, there must always be a day, even an hour and a minute, when some significant action is performed for the first or for the last time) that saw the last roll pulled down from the library shelves, the last fire dwindling in the bathroom furnaces, the death of the last landowner who " knew his Virgil " and could trace his descent back to an Augustan consul, though his own language was polluted with barbaric idiom and though his sons and grandsons were indistinguishable from Gothic squires.

Stranger yet and more perplexing the intermediate stage! Starting off from Symmachus, Ausonius and Sidonius, as they emerge through the dense yet lucid medium of Dill's late-Victorian prose style, the reader's mind embarks on visionary excursions which take him now to the makeshift court of Ravenna, infested by a swarm of greedy monks and made more noisome by pestilential waterways; now to the military headquarters of that fanatical Goth, the Arian Euric, whose governor was a Catholic named Count Victorius, and whose secretary-of-state and chief minister, the humane and accomplished classicist Leo; now to the hermitage of the holy Jerome, who, himself a finished product of the Roman schools, had put the classics behind him as works of the Devil and praised the filth-encrusted piety of St. Anthony's followers. Yet the old Roman spirit was not quite dead. Emperor after emperor—appearing and vanishing in rapid succession— issued edicts to his subordinates throughout the Empire, which reveal both the energy and the impotence of the imperial government. And as a feeling of helplessness increased at the centre, so did the measures adopted by the Emperor grow more and more ferocious, and the life and liberty of the individual decline in value. Brigandage on the part of the embittered poor, ruthless tax evasion by wealthy landlords, the flight of the middle class from bureaucratic tyranny—all were symptoms of a profound change in the body of the Empire which involved both economic life and personal standards; and pleas and rescripts and spasmodic severity did nothing to check them. . . . Dill's treatment of his period has an historical and, from the point of view of the contemporary reader, even a somewhat pathetic, interest. Since he wrote of an age of steady decline in an era of apparently continuous progress, many of his comments are as disconcerting as they are unexpected. " Persecution of any opinion or religious practice, however false, by sheer force is not a pleasant subject of contemplation to the modern mind," he remarks from the safe altitude of 1898 when describing the fierce strife of Pagan and Christian. Alas, the modern mind has grown far tougher in the last decade or so! That the enfranchisement of the individual might be a temporary blessing, and the return of darkness across Europe a recurrent phenomenon, were possibilities historians and men of letters had not yet digested.

THE END